Collins

English Expert

COURSEBOOK 3

Name: ....

Grade: ....   Section: ....

I am an ancient collection of Indian fables. I was originally written in Sanskrit more than 2000 years ago. My stories usually have animals as their main characters and teach us good values.

What is my name? ....

Renu Viswanath | Paromita Roy

HarperCollins*Publishers*

Publishing operations in 17 countries and 120+ imprints globally

William Collins' dream of knowledge for all began with the publication of his first book in 1819. A self-educated mill worker, he not only enriched millions of lives, but also founded a flourishing publishing house. Today, staying true to this spirit, Collins books are packed with inspiration, innovation and practical expertise. They place you at the centre of a world of possibility and give you exactly what you need to explore it.

Published by Collins Learning
An imprint of HarperCollins*Publishers* India
Building No. 10, Tower A, 4th Floor, DLF Cyber City, Gurugram, Haryana 122002, India

First edition: 2024
Reprint edition: 2025
ISBN: 978-93-6213-565-0

The publishers would like to thank the following reviewers for their suggestions and inputs:

Renu Arora
Saint Margaret Senior Secondary School, New Delhi

Shalini Sharma
Mother's International School

Radhika Tadepalli
Principal,
Modern Academy Senior Secondary School, Ghaziabad

Printed and bound by Thomson Press India Ltd

Browse the complete Collins catalogue at www.collins.in.
For any queries/feedback, please write to us at SCHOOLSUPPORT@harpercollins.co.in.

Preface

English Expert is a new multi-skill course in English that aims to address the needs of the learners, as underlined in the National Curriculum Framework (NCF) 2023, one of whose underlying principles is a concerted shift towards competency-based learning. This series is distinct in its inclusion of curricular goals, mapped to the respective competencies outlined by the new NCF. It focuses on literacy through thoughtfully curated content, exercises, and activities that will help to develop the 3Hs – Curious Heads, Skilled Hands, and Compassionate Hearts.

Grades 1, 3, and 6 include bridge chapters that act as a pedagogical link between the Foundational, Middle, and the Preparatory Stages. The formal requirements of language are integrated with the appreciation of literature-rich content. This is done through a combination of the communicative and the language-through-literature approaches towards language acquisition.

Care has been taken to include India-focused content and activities adhering to the principles of experiential learning and mindfulness. Additionally, the series aims to develop 21st century skills and awareness about the United Nations' Sustainable Development Goals in learners. It also fosters art integration through activities.

Coursebooks 1–8 comprise a mix of prose, poetry, and drama authored by Indian and global writers, based on themes like self and family, climate change, gender, and inclusivity. The exercises include factual, analytical, life skills, and value-based questions. Grades 6–8 include a HOTS-based comprehension section, in keeping with the latest assessment pattern. A self-assessment at the beginning of Coursebooks 2–8 acts as a useful diagnostic tool.

Language Companions 1–8 comprise extensive reading comprehension, composition, and integrated grammar and vocabulary tasks. It is designed for practice and reinforcement of the concepts taught in the Coursebooks. All topics are mapped to the respective Coursebooks and can be used for independent practice. The Language Companions for classes 3 to 8 also include SAFAL (Structured Assessments for Analyzing Learning) assessments.

Supplementary Readers 1–8 have been designed in keeping with the NCF's focus on 'drop everything and read'. The simple yet high-quality reading material has been curated to inculcate the habit of reading in learners. These books will introduce them to a wide variety of literary genres by both Indian and global authors.

Teacher's Resource Books 1–8 contain lesson plans, additional worksheets, listening transcripts for listening exercises, and answer keys for the Coursebooks, Language Companions, and additional worksheets.

Collins DigiSuite 1–8 comprises multimedia e-books, animations of the reading passages in the Coursebooks, interactivities based on the vocabulary and grammar sections, and a Test Generator for the creation of customized assignments and question papers.

Icons The series prepares learners with the various skills outlined in the NCF 2023. These are tagged with easily recognizable icons.

Twenty-first Century Skills ensure that today's students can thrive in an ever-changing world.

Collaboration · Communication · Creativity · Critical Thinking · Initiative · Leadership · Media Literacy · Productivity · Flexibility · Information Literacy · Social Skills · Technology Literacy · Innovation

India-Focused content puts the spotlight on the heritage, culture, customs, history and geography of the Indian subcontinent.

Art Integrated Learning is a pedagogic model that integrates the fine arts, performing arts, and photography into teaching.

The **Sustainable Development Goals**, adopted by the United Nations in 2015, are a collection of 17 inter-linked goals designed to achieve a sustainable future for all by 2030.

SUSTAINABLE DEVELOPMENT GOALS

Key Features

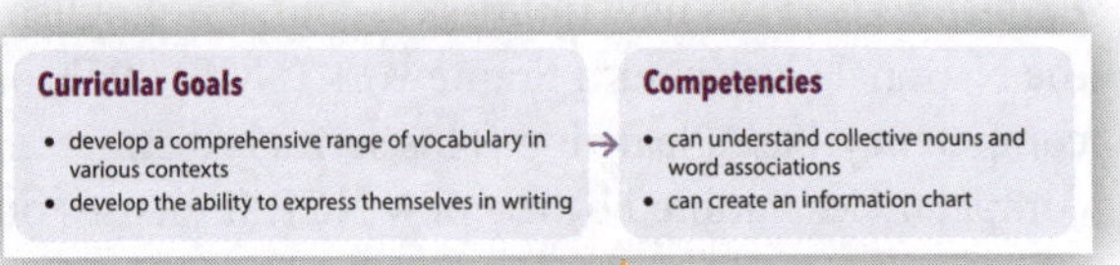
Curricular Goals
- develop a comprehensive range of vocabulary in various contexts
- develop the ability to express themselves in writing

Competencies
- can understand collective nouns and word associations
- can create an information chart

Warm-up

A. Colour the picture. If you think the lion likes to live in the forest, colour the bars brown. Draw green leaves on the bars. If you think it likes to live in the zoo, colour the bars grey.

B. Animals that we keep at home or in farms are called domestic animals. Some of them also give us food. Fill in the missing letters and name these animals.

1. __OW 2. __UCK 3. __EN 4. HO__SE

Warm-up has theme-based activities.

Curricular Goals are mapped to the respective **Competencies** outlined in the NCF 2023.

Reading comprises a rich variety of texts by global and Indian writers.

All reading passages are accompanied by an animation in **DigiSuite** and tagged by an icon.

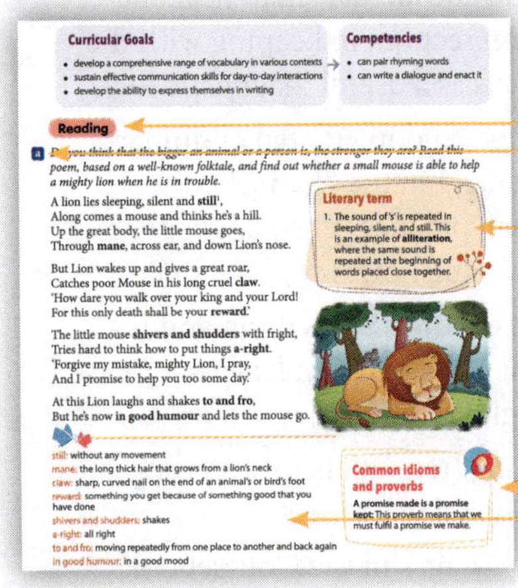
Curricular Goals
- develop a comprehensive range of vocabulary in various contexts
- sustain effective communication skills for day-to-day interactions
- develop the ability to express themselves in writing

Competencies
- can pair rhyming words
- can write a dialogue and enact it

Reading

Do you think that the bigger an animal or a person is, the stronger they are? Read this poem, based on a well-known folktale, and find out whether a small mouse is able to help a mighty lion when he is in trouble.

A lion lies sleeping, silent and **still**,
Along comes a mouse and thinks he's a hill.
Up the great body, the little mouse goes,
Through **mane**, across ear, and down Lion's nose.

But Lion wakes up and gives a great roar,
Catches poor Mouse in his long cruel **claw**.
'How dare you walk over your king and your Lord!
For this only death shall be your **reward**.'

The little mouse **shivers and shudders** with fright,
Tries hard to think how to put things **a-right**.
'Forgive my mistake, mighty Lion, I pray,
And I promise to help you too some day.'

At this Lion laughs and shakes **to and fro**,
But he's now in **good humour** and lets the mouse go.

Literary term
1. The sound of 's' is repeated in sleeping, silent, and still. This is an example of **alliteration**, where the same sound is repeated at the beginning of words placed close together.

Common idioms and proverbs
A promise made is a promise kept: This proverb means that we must fulfil a promise we make.

still: without any movement
mane: the long thick hair that grows from a lion's neck
claw: sharp, curved nail on the end of an animal's or bird's foot
reward: something you get because of something good that you have done
shivers and shudders: shakes
a-right: all right
to and fro: moving repeatedly from one place to another and back again
in good humour: in a good mood

Cross-curricular corner, Literary terms, Common idioms and proverbs have additional trivia, explanations of figures of speech, and idiomatic structures.

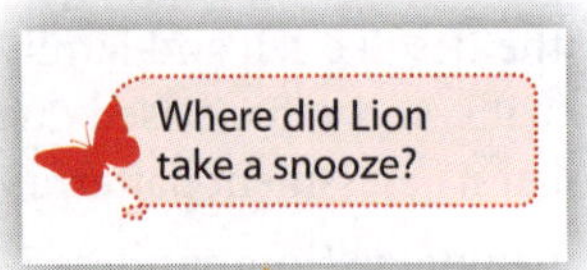
Where did Lion take a snooze?

While-reading **in-text questions** check factual understanding.

Glossary includes contextual meanings of difficult words.

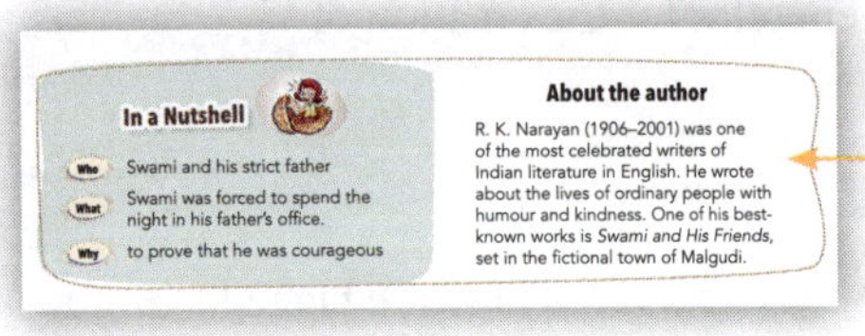
In a Nutshell
- Who: Swami and his strict father
- What: Swami was forced to spend the night in his father's office.
- Why: to prove that he was courageous

About the author

R. K. Narayan (1906–2001) was one of the most celebrated writers of Indian literature in English. He wrote about the lives of ordinary people with humour and kindness. One of his best-known works is *Swami and His Friends*, set in the fictional town of Malgudi.

In a Nutshell is a useful revision tool which recapitulates the key aspects of the text.

About the author/poet/playwright includes a brief biography of the author/poet.

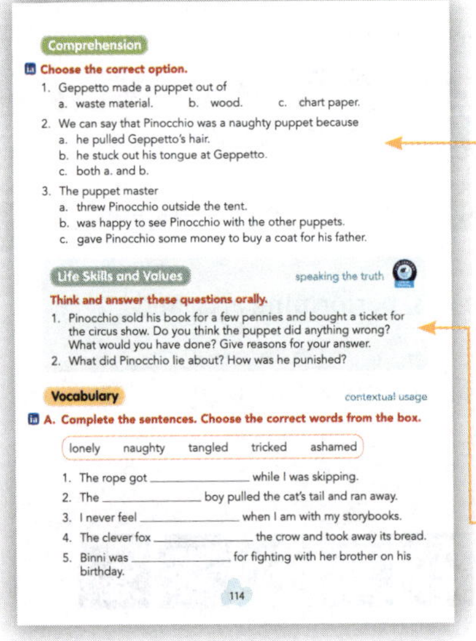
Comprehension

Choose the correct option.
1. Geppetto made a puppet out of
   a. waste material. b. wood. c. chart paper.
2. We can say that Pinocchio was a naughty puppet because
   a. he pulled Geppetto's hair.
   b. he stuck out his tongue at Geppetto.
   c. both a. and b.
3. The puppet master
   a. threw Pinocchio outside the tent.
   b. was happy to see Pinocchio with the other puppets.
   c. gave Pinocchio some money to buy a coat for his father.

Life Skills and Values — speaking the truth

Think and answer these questions orally.
1. Pinocchio sold his book for a few pennies and bought a ticket for the circus show. Do you think the puppet did anything wrong? What would you have done? Give reasons for your answer.
2. What did Pinocchio lie about? How was he punished?

Vocabulary — contextual usage

A. Complete the sentences. Choose the correct words from the box.

lonely naughty tangled tricked ashamed

1. The rope got __________ while I was skipping.
2. The __________ boy pulled the cat's tail and ran away.
3. I never feel __________ when I am with my storybooks.
4. The clever fox __________ the crow and took away its bread.
5. Binni was __________ for fighting with her brother on his birthday.

114

Comprehension checks factual understanding through 'wh-' and objective questions of various types.

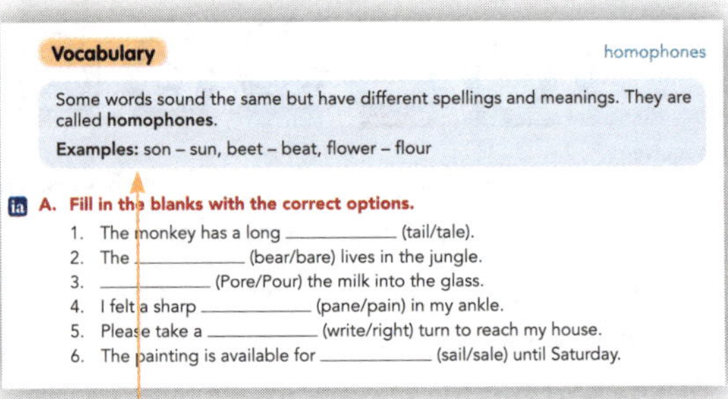
Vocabulary — homophones

Some words sound the same but have different spellings and meanings. They are called **homophones**.

Examples: son – sun, beet – beat, flower – flour

A. Fill in the blanks with the correct options.
1. The monkey has a long __________ (tail/tale).
2. The __________ (bear/bare) lives in the jungle.
3. __________ (Pore/Pour) the milk into the glass.
4. I felt a sharp __________ (pane/pain) in my ankle.
5. Please take a __________ (write/right) turn to reach my house.
6. The painting is available for __________ (sail/sale) until Saturday.

Life Skills and Values has inferential questions on values and interpersonal skills.

Vocabulary includes exercises on contextual usage, modes of language acquisition and figures of speech.

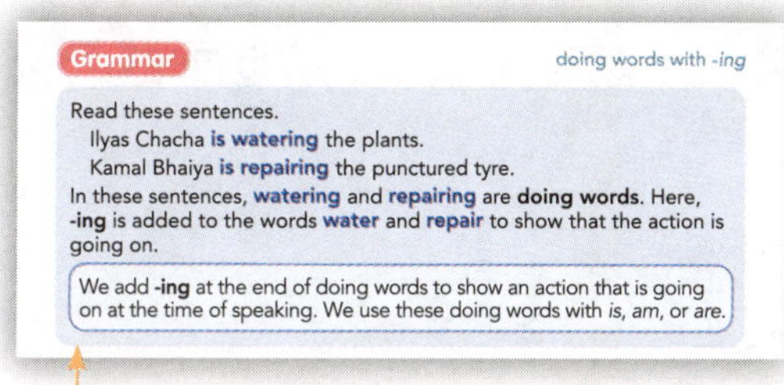

Grammar — doing words with *-ing*

Read these sentences.
Ilyas Chacha **is watering** the plants.
Kamal Bhaiya **is repairing** the punctured tyre.
In these sentences, **watering** and **repairing** are **doing words**. Here, **-ing** is added to the words **water** and **repair** to show that the action is going on.

We add **-ing** at the end of doing words to show an action that is going on at the time of speaking. We use these doing words with *is*, *am*, or *are*.

Grammar includes graded practice tasks accompanied by simple explanations.

Study Skills includes graded phonics, spelling, and dictionary activities.

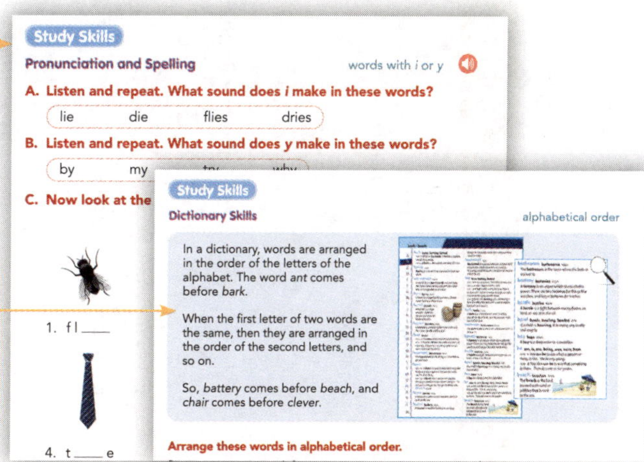

Study Skills

Pronunciation and Spelling — words with *i* or *y*

A. Listen and repeat. What sound does *i* make in these words?

lie die flies dries

B. Listen and repeat. What sound does *y* make in these words?

by my

C. Now look at the

1. fl____

4. t____e

Study Skills

Dictionary Skills — alphabetical order

In a dictionary, words are arranged in the order of the letters of the alphabet. The word *ant* comes before *bark*.

When the first letter of two words are the same, then they are arranged in the order of the second letters, and so on.

So, *battery* comes before *beach*, and *chair* comes before *clever*.

Arrange these words in alphabetical order.

B. How does each member of the family help Bala's mother? Look at the pictures. Match each picture with the person.

Grandpa Father Grandma Bala

Exercises available as interactivities on **DigiSuite** are tagged with an icon.

Listening covers aural comprehension activities, as well as word and sentence-based **Dictation** tasks.

Speaking includes role plays, conversation practice and public speaking tasks through solo, pair and group work. It also covers financial literacy tasks.

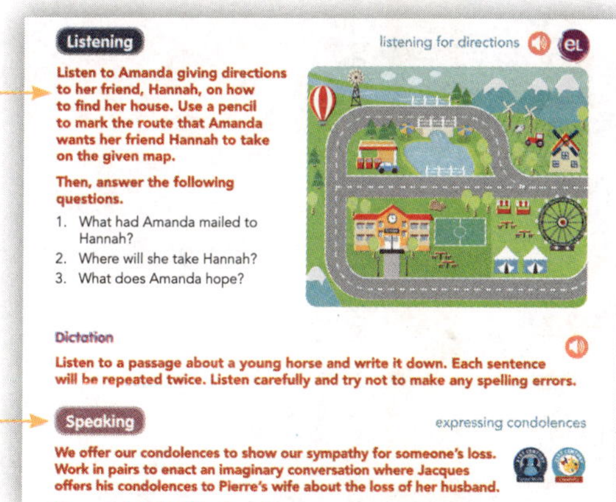

Listening — listening for directions

Listen to Amanda giving directions to her friend, Hannah, on how to find her house. Use a pencil to mark the route that Amanda wants her friend Hannah to take on the given map.

Then, answer the following questions.

1. What had Amanda mailed to Hannah?
2. Where will she take Hannah?
3. What does Amanda hope?

Dictation

Listen to a passage about a young horse and write it down. Each sentence will be repeated twice. Listen carefully and try not to make any spelling errors.

Speaking — expressing condolences

We offer our condolences to show our sympathy for someone's loss. Work in pairs to enact an imaginary conversation where Jacques offers his condolences to Pierre's wife about the loss of her husband.

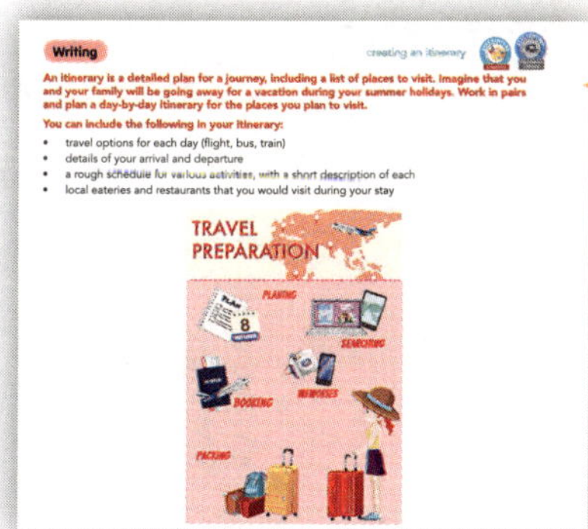

Writing — creating an itinerary

An itinerary is a detailed plan for a journey, including a list of places to visit. Imagine that you and your family will be going away for a vacation during your summer holidays. Work in pairs and plan a day-by-day itinerary for the places you plan to visit.

You can include the following in your itinerary:

- travel options for each day (flight, bus, train)
- details of your arrival and departure
- a rough schedule for various activities, with a short description of each
- local eateries and restaurants that you would visit during your stay

Writing includes graded and free composition. Poetry chapters include **Activity**, a hands-on creative task.

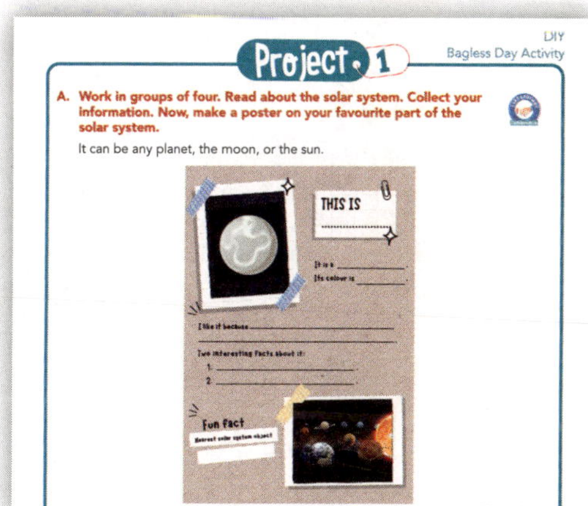

Project 1 — DIY Bagless Day Activity

A. Work in groups of four. Read about the solar system. Collect your information. Now, make a poster on your favourite part of the solar system.

It can be any planet, the moon, or the sun.

Explore More

Read the book *Animal Stories for Children* by Ruskin Bond. It is a collection of stories about funny animals and their adventures.

Watch the film *The Amazing Panda Adventure*. It shows the adventures of a young boy and a panda.

Listen to the song *My Best Friend* by Heidi Winzinger. It talks about the friendship between a dog and its owner.

Explore More has suggestions for further reading, watching and listening to encourage learners to delve further into the theme of the reading text.

Projects cover cross-curricular activities aligned to the unit themes. They also include 'bagless day' activities.

Detailed Contents

Unit	Chapter Name	Reading Comprehension	Vocabulary	Grammar	Study Skills	Listening	Speaking	Writing	Activity
I. Secrets of the Sky	1. Rathna and the Ring of Fire	• Sequencing and summarising • Factual, inferential, and extrapolative questions	• Crossword	• Revision of common and proper nouns • Countable and uncountable nouns: usage of *a*, *an*, *some* • Personal and possessive pronouns	• Pronunciation: silent letters	• Listening to a passage and stating true or false	• Asking and answering *yes/no* questions	• Writing a narrative paragraph	
	2. *The Star*	• MCQ • Factual, inferential, and extrapolative questions	• Adjectives • Rhyming words						• Recitation
II. Healthy and Good Habits	3. Superfoods for Superheroes	• Gap filling • Factual, inferential, and extrapolative questions	• Phrasal verbs • Plurals of words ending with *-y* and *-f*	• Simple present and past tenses • Usage of *do/does* • Usage of *has, have, had*	• Spelling: words with *ll*	• Listening to a recipe and sequencing	• Speaking on a given topic	• Writing a process	
	4. *Litterbug*	• MCQ • Reference to context • Inferential and extrapolative questions	• Synonyms • Antonyms						• Making a collage • Writing a paragraph
	5. The Porridge Pincher	• Completing a table • Factual, inferential, and extrapolative questions	• One word, two meanings	• Usage of *some, a lot of, any, a few, many, much* • Usage of *can, may, might, could, should, would*	• Dictionary skills: alphabetical order	• Listening to a description and drawing	• Role play: an interview	• Sharing your feelings	
Project 1 (DIY and bagless day activity) • Making a poster • Making a mural to create awareness on cleanliness									
III. Nature Around Us	6. A Butterfly Smile	• Sequencing • Factual, inferential, and extrapolative questions	• Similes • Words related to movement	• Functions of adjectives • Comparison of adjectives • Reflexive pronouns: *myself, yourself, himself, herself*	• Spelling: forming plurals	• Listening to a poem followed by gap filling • Dictation	• Role play: introducing yourself	• Writing an informal letter	
	7. *The Wind*	• MCQ • Reference to context • Inferential and extrapolative questions	• Word grid • Making sentences						• Picture composition

IV. Humour	8. Drip, Drip	• MCQ • Reference to context • Inferential and extrapolative questions	• Homophones • Word pairs	• Nouns: plural and possessives • Collective nouns • Prepositions of position and time	• Pronunciation: sounds of homophones	• Listening to a passage and gap filling	• Narrating a story with picture clues	• Writing in the past tense	
	9. *The Green Hedgehog*	• Factual, inferential, and extrapolative questions	• Collocations • Homographs						• Pictogram • Writing a funny poem
Project 2 (DIY and bagless day activity) • Making a booklet • Dumb charades									
V. Friends and Family	10. Paplu, the Giant	• Completing a flowchart • Reference to context • Inferential and extrapolative questions	• Contextual usage • Sound words	• Subject and predicate • Conjunctions: *and, but, so, or*	• Pronunciation: hard and soft sounds of *g*	• Listening to a passage and stating true or false • Dictation of simple sentences	• Role play: asking for and offering help	• Making a poster	
	11. Brown Bear and Wilbur Wolf	• Factual, inferential, and extrapolative questions	• Compound words • Suffixes	• Adverbs • Negative sentences • Punctuation: comma, full stop, capital letters	• Spelling: Suffix *-tion*	• Listening to a passage and answering questions • Dictation of a short passage	• Completing a dialogue	• Writing notices for *Lost* and *Wanted*	
	12. Heidi Meets Grandfather	• Completing sentences • Inferential and extrapolative questions	• Antonyms • Collocations	• Subject–verb agreement • Articles	• Spelling: Jumbled words	• Listening to a passage followed by gap filling	• Making polite requests and thanking someone	• Describing the similarities and differences between two pictures	
VI. Folktales	13. *The Lion and the Mouse*	• True and false • Reference to context • Inferential and extrapolative questions	• Rhyming words						• Writing a dialogue, making and enacting it with sock puppets
	14. Gopal and the Hilsa Fish	• True and false • Reference to context • Inferential and extrapolative questions	• Phrasal verbs • Prefixes: *un-, in-, dis-*	• Subject–verb–object • Apostrophe in contractions	• Spelling: correcting common mistakes	• Listening to a folktale for details	• Extempore speaking / just a minute (JAM)	• Writing a diary entry	
	15. True Friends	• True and false • Reference to context • Inferential and extrapolative questions	• Synonyms • Using *get, make, have, let*	• Present continuous and past continuous tenses • Simple future tense • Simple commands and instructions	• Pronunciation: sounds of *v* and *w*	• Listening to and identifying polite and rude commands	• Giving simple instructions	• Writing a narrative paragraph	
Project 3 (Bagless day activities) • Conducting an interview • Writing a book review									

Contents

Self-Assessment 9

Unit I: Secrets of the Sky **11**

1. Rathna and the Ring of Fire by Nandita Jayaraj 12
2. *The Star* by Jane Taylor 23

Unit II: Healthy and Good Habits **27**

3. Superfoods for Superheroes by Namita Moolani Mehra 28
4. *Litterbug* by Ray Mather 37
5. The Porridge Pincher by David Wood 41

Project 1 **52**

Unit III: Nature Around Us **53**

6. A Butterfly Smile by Mathangi Subramanian 54
7. *The Wind* by Paul King 64

Unit IV: Humour **68**

8. Drip, Drip by Alka Shankar and Sharleen Mukundan 69
9. *The Green Hedgehog* by Celia Warren 78

Project 2 **83**

Unit V: Friends and Family **84**

10. Paplu, the Giant by Ramendra Kumar 85
11. Brown Bear and Wilbur Wolf by Sarah Parry 96
12. Heidi Meets Grandfather by Johanna Spyri 106

Unit VI: Folktales **115**

13. *The Lion and the Mouse* by Paul King 116
14. Gopal and the Hilsa Fish 121
15. True Friends 128

Project 3 **136**

Self-Assessment

A. Fill in the blanks with the opposites of the underlined words. (4 × 0.5)

1. It is <u>day</u> in India, but ________ in America.
2. I <u>lost</u> my pencil. Then, I ________ it under the table.
3. His name, Krishnakumar, is <u>long</u>. We made it ________ and call him Krish.
4. My shoes are <u>clean</u> when I go to school. They are ________ when I get back home.

B. Write the plurals of the given words using *s* or *es*. (6 × 1)

Column A	Column B
1. box	a.
2. plate	b.
3. match	c.
4. brush	d.
5. bottle	e.
6. tomato	f.

C. Circle the describing words that go with the given nouns. (5 × 1)

1. I sat in the shade of a long/tall **tree**.
2. I was tired and went into a deep/lazy **sleep**.
3. There was a thick/wide **road** along the beach.
4. The weather report says there will be heavy/great **rain**.
5. My grandmother likes to start her day with a cup of strong/powerful **coffee**.

D. Fill in the blanks with the correct position words. (6 × 0.5)

under   between   in   on   at   over

1. The cat hid ____________ the table when it heard the dog bark.
2. I usually go to school ____________ 8:00 a.m.
3. I sat ____________ my friend and my sister.
4. There was a spider ____________ the wall.
5. There is milk ____________ the fridge.
6. The birds flew ____________ the tree.

E. Complete the sentences with the correct pronouns from the box. (8 × 0.5)

you/your	he/his	I/my	we/our

1. _______ love _______ new home.
2. _______ am going to tell _______ story.
3. _______ is practising for _______ driving test.
4. _______ need to put away all _______ toys before going to bed.

F. Fill in the blanks with the correct forms of the verbs in brackets. (10 × 1)

1. My sister is very tired. She _______________ (rest).
2. This morning, Radha _______________ (slip) and _______________ (fall).
3. Ritika _______________ (eat) her food very quickly. She was very hungry.
4. Jiby is late for school. He _______________ (run) to the bus stop.
5. When I reached my friend's place, she _______________ (write) her essay.
6. Deepti _______________ (sit) in class. She does not _______________ (like) to miss school.
7. My mother _______________ (start) her new job last month. She _______________ (go) to office every day.

The answers are given on page 82.

Assessment

1. If you score equal to or more than what is marked below, you are ready to start the new chapters.
2. If you score less than 1.5 in section A, revise 'Opposites'.
3. If you score less than 4 in section B, revise 'One and Many'.
4. If you score less than 3 in section C, revise 'Collocations'.
5. If you score less than 2 in section D, revise 'Position Words'.
6. If you score less than 3 in section E, revise 'Pronouns'.
7. If you score less than 7 in section F, revise 'Verbs'.

UNIT I

Secrets of the Sky

Warm-up

Have you ever looked up at the night sky on a clear evening? What do you see? Can you see any patterns being formed by a group of stars?

A. Draw lines to join these groups of stars. What do these shapes remind you of? Match them with their names and write the correct number in the box.

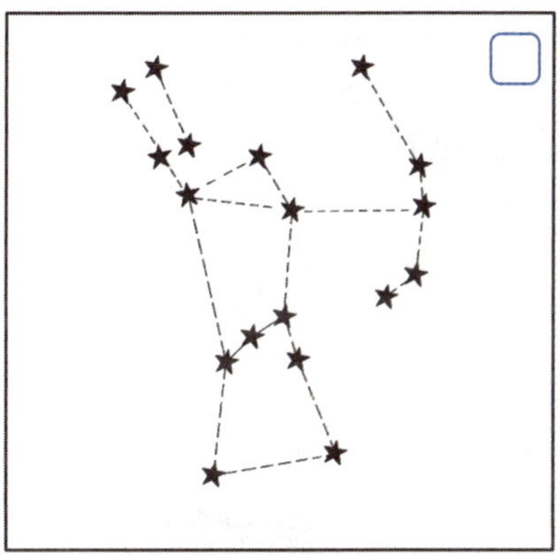

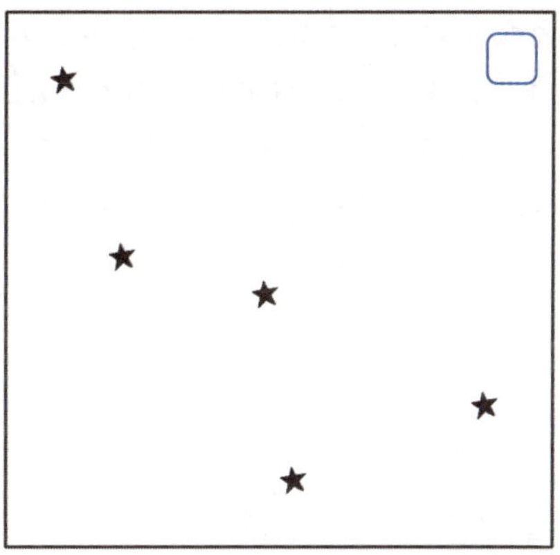

Group of stars	Looks like
1. Big Dipper	a saucepan
2. Orion	a hunter with bow and arrow
3. Cassiopeia	the letter 'W'

B. Take this quick quiz on stars and state whether the statements are true (T) or false (F).

1. The sun is a star. ☐
2. The moon is a star. ☐
3. Stars are made of cool gases. ☐
4. A large group of stars is called a galaxy. ☐
5. We can get a good look at stars through a telescope. ☐

graphic story

1

Rathna and the Ring of Fire

Nandita Jayaraj

Curricular Goals

- develop fluency in reading and the ability to read with comprehension
- sustain effective communication skills for day-to-day interactions
- develop the ability to express themselves in writing

→

Competencies

- can identify different types of nouns and pronouns and use articles correctly
- can identify silent letters in words
- can ask and answer *yes/no* questions and write a narrative paragraph

Reading

a *Have you ever been to a planetarium? This story is an account of a day in the life of Dr Nandivada Rathnashree, who was an astronomer and worked at the Nehru Planetarium in New Delhi. It's the day of the solar eclipse and hundreds of people are gathered to watch it. Read the story to find out what happens.*

Today is a day like no other. For one full minute, the sun will disappear behind the moon. There will be a thin ring of fire where a bright golden ball used to be. Today, there is a **solar eclipse**.

solar eclipse: the time when the sun gets blocked because the moon is between the Earth and the sun

Rathna is an **astronomer** at the **planetarium**. She and her friends are very excited about the solar eclipse. After all, it is a **sight** nobody should miss.

Rathna knows many secrets of the **universe**. Like what happens when a **billion**-year-old star dies. And how the sun can disappear behind the moon.

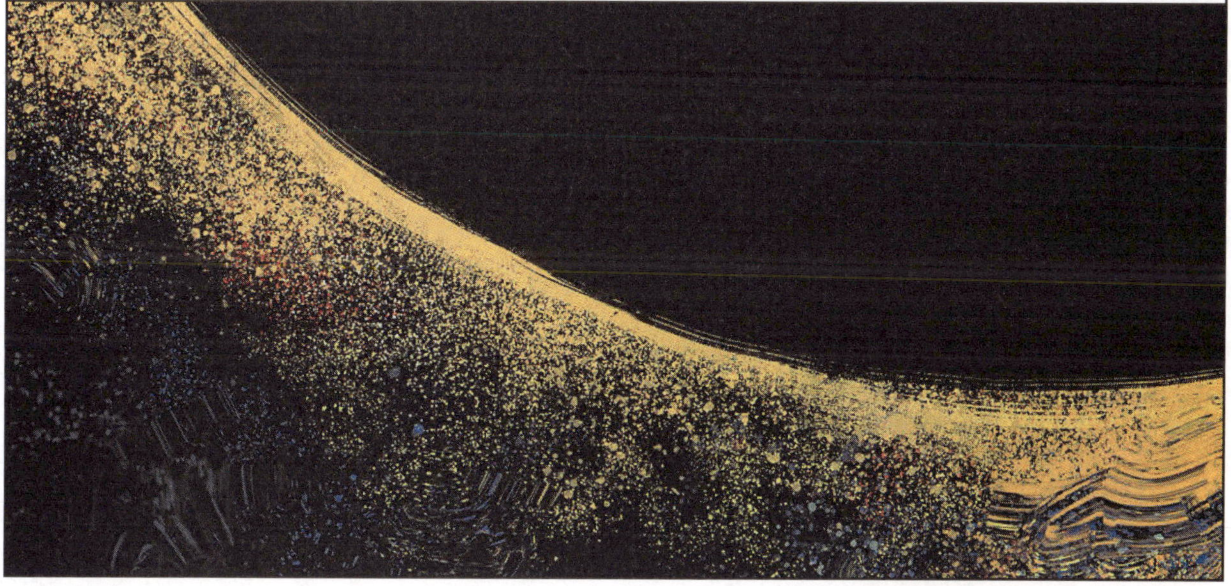

What secrets does Rathna know about the universe?

astronomer: a scientist who studies the stars, planets, and other objects in space

planetarium: a building where lights are shone on the ceiling to show how the planets and the stars move

sight: something that you see

universe: the whole of space

billion: (here) extremely old

Rathna shows people the best views of stars, planets and distant **galaxies**. Sometimes through **telescopes**. Sometimes from her sky **theatre**, and sometimes from ancient **observatories** like the Jantar Mantar.

Today, there are two hundred eclipse glasses on Rathna's table. These glasses must be worn while looking at the ring of fire. Two hundred visitors head to the telescope and **projection** boxes to take a closer look at the sky and the sun hiding behind the moon. Soon the sun is out and Rathna has another surprise in store.

Why do the visitors head to the projection boxes?

galaxies: very large groups of stars and planets to which the Earth and the solar system belong

telescopes: long tube-shaped instruments that make distant objects seem larger and nearer

theatre: a building where plays and shows take place

observatories: buildings with large telescopes from where scientists study the stars and the planets

projection: the act of making a film or a picture appear onto a screen or wall

domed: rounded

projector: a machine that makes images appear onto a screen or wall

In a Nutshell

Who Rathna, an astronomer

Where At the planetarium

What She shows secrets of the universe to the visitors.

When Day of the solar eclipse

How With special eclipse glasses

About the author

Nandita Jayaraj is a science writer. She has written many children's books. Some of them are *Rathna and the Ring of Fire*, *31 Fantastic Adventures in Science* with Aashima Dogra, and *Anna's Extraordinary Experiments with Weather*.

Comprehension

A. Complete the summary of the story using the sentences from the help box.

1. Rathna has a surprise in store for the visitors.
2. ☐
3. The sky theatre is a dark room with a domed roof.
4. ☐
5. ☐
6. The roof has turned into the night sky.
7. ☐

- There is a giant projector in the sky theatre.
- She guides them into the sky theatre.
- Rathna will now take them on a journey through space.
- The visitors lean back in their seats and look up.

B. Answer these questions.

1. What is the special sight that the story talks about?
2. How many visitors come to the planetarium?
3. Mention two things that Rathna does as an astronomer.
4. What is the special item that the visitors will need for the event?

Life Skills and Values

inspiring others

21ST CENTURY Critical Thinking

1. What are the qualities that make Rathna a good astronomer?
2. Name two skills that you would like to learn. Why?

Vocabulary

contextual usage

ia Complete the crossword using the clues given below.

Across

2. the act of travelling from one place to another
5. a scientist who studies the stars, planets, and other objects in space
6. a long instrument that has lenses to make distant things look larger and nearer
8. balls of gas that you see as small points of light in the sky
9. an extremely large group of stars and planets
10. a semi-circled spherical roof or object

Down

1. an instrument used to project a film onto a screen or wall
3. the whole of space including the stars, planets, galaxies, etc.
4. a building where lights are shone on the ceiling to show how the planets and the stars move
7. an occasion when the moon or the sun seems to completely or partly disappear

Grammar

Look at the nouns in these sentences.

Rathna is an **astronomer**.

She works at the **planetarium**.

Some nouns are the general names of a person, place, or thing. These are called **common nouns**.

The nouns *astronomer* and *planetarium* are common nouns.

Some nouns are special names given to a person, place, animal, or thing. These are called **proper nouns**. Proper nouns begin with a capital letter.

The word *Rathna* is a proper noun.

A. Circle the common nouns and underline the proper nouns.

1. Meet my dog, Woofer!
2. The area outside Earth is space.
3. Enid Blyton was an English writer.
4. Wednesday is a good day to start your work.
5. Jupiter is the largest planet of the solar system.

countable and uncountable nouns

Look at the nouns in this sentence.

Rathna took the **visitors** to the dark **room**.

Here, the nouns *visitors* and *room* can be counted. (*200 visitors, one room*)

Countable nouns are names of things that can be counted.

Now, read this sentence.

She showed them the **sky**.

The noun *sky* cannot be counted.
It is an uncountable noun.

Language Booster

Hair is a word that can be used as both countable and uncountable nouns.

Uncountable nouns are names of things that cannot be counted.

B. Read these sentences and write the underlined nouns in the correct columns.

1. The sky is vast.
2. Fruit juice is good for health.
3. There are many trees in the park.
4. The tomatoes were red and fresh.
5. I have added some salt to the soup.
6. There are many galaxies in the universe.

Countable nouns	Uncountable nouns

a, an, some

A is used before a countable noun that is singular and begins with a consonant sound.

Example: **A** *bird* flew out of its nest. (The noun *bird* is one in number and begins with a consonant sound.)

An is used with a countable noun that is singular and begins with a vowel sound.

Example: **An** *alien* landed on Earth. (The noun *alien* is one in number and begins with a vowel sound.)

Some can be used with plural countable nouns and uncountable nouns.

Examples: There are **some** *stars* that are closer to Earth than others. (The noun *stars* is a plural countable noun.)

There is **some** *water* in the jug. (The noun *water* is an uncountable noun.)

C. Fill in the blanks with *a, an,* or *some.*

1. ________ sand got into my shoe at the beach. I will need ________ help to remove it. May I borrow ________ pair of shoes from you till mine dries out? Let's have ________ glass of lemonade while cleaning up.
2. We need ________ apple soaked in syrup, ________ plums, ________ scoop each of almonds and walnuts, ________ flour, ________ dozen eggs, and ________ enormous baking tray before we bake. ________ van will arrive in ________ hour to pick up the delivery. I am going to need ________ help from all of you.

We use **personal pronouns** (*I, me, he, him, she, her, you, us, etc.*) in place of common nouns or proper nouns.

Example: Rathna gets many visitors. **She** is an astronomer.

(*She* stands for *Rathna.*)

We use **possessive pronouns** (*mine, ours, yours, hers, his, their*) to show that something belongs to someone. They are used in the place of nouns that show belonging.

Example: The **visitors** head to the telescope boxes. The glasses were **theirs**.

(*Theirs* stands for *the visitors.*)

ia **D. Fill in the blanks with suitable pronouns. Choose from the list given in the box. Some may be repeated.**

I	you	he	it	we	us	its
mine	his	yours	theirs	ours		

1. Arish saw the neighbour's dog running in the park. __________ is running loose on its own. __________ had to make sure it was __________, before chasing __________.
2. The house is __________ and __________ paint is flaking. __________ need to call the repairman immediately to fix __________. The guests are coming next month. The decision to stay with __________ was __________ but to keep it fresh and welcoming is __________.
3. __________ made some cheesecake for dessert. It is for __________ and those guests of __________. __________ can have coffee later in the garden. That would be the perfect ending for this visit of __________.

Study Skills

Pronunciation

silent letters

Listen to the words and repeat them as you listen. Circle the silent letter(s) in each word. Write them in the correct columns in the table. Then, say the words aloud with the correct pronunciation.

1. knife	3. calm	5. talk	7. column	9. autumn	11. sign
2. knock	4. walk	6. foreign	8. knee	10. design	12. hymn

Silent *g*	Silent *k*	Silent *l*	Silent *n*

Now, add one word of your own in each box.

Listening

listening to a passage and stating true or false

Listen to the passage and state whether the statements are true (T) or false (F).

1. Dr Rathnashree was born in Delhi. ☐
2. She joined the Nehru Planetarium in 1996. ☐
3. She worked in laboratories only in Hyderabad. ☐
4. She could never become the director of Nehru Planetarium. ☐
5. She took part in the restoration of the Jantar Mantar at Delhi and Jaipur. ☐
6. She became the director of the Astronomical Society of India. ☐
7. Dr Rathnashree was a famous astrology educator of India. ☐
8. Dr Rathnashree passed away from COVID-19 in 2021. ☐

Speaking

asking and answering *yes/no* questions

A. In pairs, enact these short conversations. Take turns to ask and answer the questions using 'Yes' or 'No'.

Father: Would you like to visit the planetarium?
Rahul: Yes, I would.

Tamal: Did you watch the night sky in the domed room?
Alam: No, I didn't.

B. Now, complete and enact these conversations.

1. Have you cleaned your room?
2. Did you lose the keys?
3. Should I pack your bag?

Writing

writing a narrative paragraph

Imagine you have visited a planetarium/adventure camp/zoo/wildlife sanctuary. Write a paragraph about your experience in your notebook.

You can write about these:

- where and when you went
- who you went with
- what you saw there or what you did
- how the visit ended and how you felt

Explore More

Read the story *Tara Finds her Stars* by Mala Kumar and Manisha Chaudhry. Tara is a girl who likes to sleep under the stars. Read the story to know about her exciting journey.

Watch the film *E.T. the Extra-Terrestrial*. It is the story about a young boy who tries to help an alien return to his home.

Listen to the song *The Eight Planets* by JunyTony. It is a song about all the planets of the solar system.

poem 2

The Star

Jane Taylor

Curricular Goals

- develop a comprehensive range of vocabulary in various contexts
- sustain effective communication skills for day-to-day interactions

→

Competencies

- can understand adjectives and pair rhyming words
- can recite a poem

Reading

a *Have you ever looked at the sky and wondered how far away from us the stars are? Though far away, stars brighten the night with their light. Read this poem about the way a small star's light shines far and wide. The first stanza of the poem is a well-known nursery rhyme.*

Twinkle, twinkle, little star,
How I **wonder** what you are!
Up above the world so high,
Like a diamond in the sky.[1]

When the **blazing** sun is gone,
When he nothing shines upon,
Then you show your little light,
Twinkle, twinkle, all the night.

In the dark blue sky you **keep**,
And often through my curtains **peep**,
For you never shut your eye,
Till the sun is in the sky.

So the traveller in the dark,
Thanks you for your tiny **spark**,
He could not see which way to go,
If you did not twinkle so.

Literary term

1. This is a **simile**. The poet is comparing the twinkling star to a bright glittering diamond using the word *like*.

wonder: to think about something
blazing: burning or shining brightly
keep: to stay
peep: have a quick look at something in secret
spark: (here) light

In a Nutshell

Who A tiny star

When From sunset to sunrise

What It twinkles in the night sky and helps the traveller find his way.

About the poet

Jane Taylor (1783–1824) was an English poet and novelist. She and her sister Ann wrote poems together. The poem you just read is from their book *Rhymes for the Nursery*.

Understanding the Poem

A. Choose the correct meanings of the following lines from the poem.

1. *Up above the world so high,*
   - a. The star is just above the ground.
   - b. The star can be seen high up in the sky.
   - c. The star can be seen above the mountains.
2. *When he nothing shines upon,*
   - a. When the sun shines brightly.
   - b. When the sun sets.
   - c. When the star stops shining.
3. *For you never shut your eye*
   Till the sun is in the sky.
   - a. The star never wakes up during the day.
   - b. The sun does not sleep until the star comes out.
   - c. The star can be seen in the sky until the sun comes up.
4. *He could not see which way to go,*
   - a. The traveller did not know the way.
   - b. The traveller could not see in the dark.
   - c. The traveller had lost his way.

B. Answer these questions in one or two lines.

1. What does the little star in the sky look like?
2. Who do you think is the 'I' in the poem?
3. Why is the sun described as 'blazing'?

4. When does the star shut its eye?
5. Who do you think is the 'traveller in the dark'?

Life Skills and Values helping others

Critical Thinking

In the poem, the star helps the traveller find his way in the dark. You can also help someone when they need you. Think of two ways in which you can be like the little spark of light for someone at these places.

1. in school/class
2. at home

Vocabulary

adjectives

We use adjectives to describe people and things.

Examples: **tired** traveller (The word *tired* describes the person *traveller*.)
little star (The word *little* describes the thing *star*.)

A. Do these words describe people or things? Write *P* for person and *T* for thing.

1. smart ____________
2. expensive ____________
3. sad ____________
4. red ____________
5. short ____________
6. hungry ____________
7. long ____________
8. old ____________

rhyming words

Look at these lines from the poem.

In the dark blue sky you **keep**,
And often through my curtains **peep**,
For you never shut your **eye**,
Till the sun is in the **sky**.

The words *keep–peep* and *eye–sky* are similar in sound.
They are **rhyming words**.

B. Complete the following sentences by pairing the last word with the correct rhyming word.

1. The sky is filled with light.
   That is so, so ________________ (right/night/bright).

2. I am going to ______________ (pray/stay/bray).
   So, I have more time to play.
3. We just had a difficult test.
   So, I will now go and ______________ (nest/digest/rest).
4. It is too hot to play because it is noon.
   Mummy is going to yell, 'Come home ______________ (moon/soon/boon).'

Activity

recitation

A. Recite the poem 'The Star' with proper expressions.

B. Look up another poem on a star in your library and recite it in class.

Explore More

Read the poem *My Glow-in-the-Dark Bedroom* by Celia Warren. A child talks about all the glow-in-the-dark objects he has in his room.

Watch the film *Mars Needs Moms*. It tells the story of a boy named Milo. His mother gets kidnapped by aliens and Milo boards a Martian spaceship to save her.

UNIT II

Healthy and Good Habits

Warm-up

A. First, think of the food items that you want to eat but are not good for your health. Next, think of the healthy food items that you should eat. Then, write them in the table. The first one has been done for you.

Food items I like to eat	Food items I should eat
ice cream	*jaggery*

B. Do you see litter on the streets when you go out? How does it make you feel? How do you think tourists feel when they see litter while visiting our country? Talk about it in class. Mention two ways that the streets can be kept cleaner.

short story

3

Superfoods for Superheroes

Namita Moolani Mehra

Curricular Goals

- develop a comprehensive range of vocabulary in various contexts
- develop fluency in reading and the ability to read with comprehension
- sustain effective communication skills for day-to-day interactions
- develop the ability to express themselves in writing

→

Competencies

- can understand the use of phrasal verbs, plurals of *-y* and *-f* ending words, different tenses of verbs, and *do*, *does*, *has*, *have*, *had*
- can spell and identify words with *ll*, speak on a given topic, and write a process

Reading

a *Superhero Shivum was not well. More than missing school, he worried whether he was no longer a superhero as he was sick. Read on to find out about the 'magic' that cured him.*

SUSTAINABLE DEVELOPMENT GOALS 3 GOOD HEALTH AND WELL-BEING

'Superheroes don't get sick, do they, Papa?' sniffled Shivum as he shivered under the covers. His throat hurt and he was feeling **grumpy**. It had been a few days since he had seen his friends.

'Of course, they do! And even superheroes have to rest when they're sick,' said Papa.

> What did Shivum want to be?

'Superheroes eat lots of healing superfoods to feel super again! They also drink a special tea and magic **potion** with powerful **ingredients** in it, to get their superpowers back as quickly as possible.'

Shivum's eyes **lit up**. He wanted some of this special tea and magic potion. He couldn't really imagine superheroes sitting around and drinking tea, but Papa was usually right about everything. 'Would you like to try the magic potion?' Papa asked. Shivum nodded eagerly.

A few minutes later, Papa was back with Shivum's cup. In it was a spoonful of yellow **gooey** liquid **speckled** with tiny black bits. The potion didn't look very tasty. Seeing Shivum's crinkled nose, Papa said, 'It tastes better than it looks. Trust me! Try it!'

'What's in the potion, Papa?'

grumpy: bad-tempered and unhappy
potion: a drink that contains magic powers
ingredients: the different items you use when you are cooking a particular dish
lit up: (here) became bright, when very surprised or happy
gooey: very soft and sticky
speckled: covered with small marks, spots, or shapes

'There's a big pinch of bright yellow turmeric, the most powerful spice, which helps **heal** all the **ouchies** in your body.

Then I put in a bit of ginger, which helps lessen the pain and makes you feel stronger.

I added a **dollop** of raw honey, which fights germs and sweetens the potion.

Lastly, I **sprinkled** some freshly ground black pepper, which boosts the power of turmeric.

Then I mixed everything together while saying a secret healing spell … '

'What's the spell, Papa?'

heal: to become healthy and normal again
ouchies: (informal usage) minor injuries
dollop: a large spoonful of soft or sticky food
sprinkled: scattered some liquid or powder over something

Cross-curricular Corner

Turmeric is a powerful medicine for cuts and swellings. Many people mix turmeric in their warm milk to fight against diseases. Some even apply its paste on their body for good skin.

'Oh, precious superfoods, this is our healing spell. Restore superpowers to those who are unwell. May this magic potion give energy and powers. And make them feel much better in just a few hours!'

Shivum smiled. He drank the potion in one big **gulp**. It didn't taste too bad! He felt a tiny bit better and was now **super** sleepy. Shivum was glad he had on his favourite superhero pajamas. Surely his superpowers would be back in the morning!

gulp: a large amount of something swallowed at once

super: (here) extremely or very

In a Nutshell

Who Shivum and his father

What Shivum wanted to be a superhero but he fell sick. His father helped him.

How His father prepared a magic potion to heal him.

About the author

Namita Moolani Mehra is a children's book and cookbook author. She has published two cookbooks, a children's cookbook, and a storybook. She wrote *Superfoods for Superheroes* for both parents and children. This story is from that book.

Comprehension

A. Fill in the blanks with the given words from the story.

grumpy	potion	ingredients	lit up
gooey	speckled	dollop	sprinkled

1. Father ______________ some salt and pepper over the ______________ in the sandwich.
2. Our neighbour is a ______________ person. The children do not play near his house.
3. My eyes ______________ when I saw the beautifully wrapped gift on my bed.
4. Add a ______________ of butter to the dish. Let it melt into the gravy.
5. The heavy rain turned the track into a ______________ mess.
6. Asterix took a sip of the magic ______________ and immediately grew in strength.
7. The night sky was ______________ with stars.

B. Answer these questions.

1. When Shivum was sick, what did his father ask him to do?
2. What was in the cup? How much of it was there?
3. What did it look like?
4. What did Shivum do when he saw what was in the cup?
5. What were the ingredients that Shivum's father used?
6. What happened when he drank it?

Life Skills and Values

being a superhero

A superhero is a person with very special qualities. What kind of a superhero would you want to be? Give reasons for your answer.

Vocabulary

phrasal verbs

A **phrasal verb** is made up of a verb and another word, which together have a new meaning.

Example: He couldn't really imagine superheroes **sitting around** and drinking tea. Here, *sitting around* is a phrasal verb.

ia **A. Fill in the blanks with the correct phrasal verbs from the box.**

stay away	fill out	pick up	look after	went over	gave away

1. Please ______________ the form for your ID card.
2. We ______________ the lesson again to understand it.
3. Mother asked the children to ______________ from fire.
4. We drove to the railway station to ______________ my cousin.
5. Shivum's father stayed to ______________ him while he was unwell.
6. The magician ______________ candies to all the children at the show.

plurals of words ending with *-y* and *-f*

The nouns ending with a consonant and *-y* form their plurals by removing the *-y* and adding *-ies*.

Examples: berr**y** (consonant + *y*) → berr**ies**

bab**y** (consonant + *y*) → bab**ies**

The nouns ending with a vowel and -*y* form their plurals by adding -*s*.

Examples: boy (vowel + *y*) ➔ boys

toy (vowel + *y*) ➔ toys

The nouns ending in -*f* or -*fe* form their plurals by removing the -*f* or -*fe* and adding -*ves*.

Examples: leaf ➔ leaves

wife ➔ wives

B. Fill in the blanks with the correct plurals of the words in brackets.

1. There were no ______________ (dairy) near their house.
2. The ______________ (loaf) of bread were put in a steel trunk.
3. We divided the chocolate in two equal ______________ (half).
4. We were told to be careful of ______________ (monkey) in the camping site.
5. The night at the camp was most fun. We lit a fire and sat around it telling ______________ (story).
6. All the ______________ (knife) at his home are not sharp. He can't cut the tomatoes.

Grammar

simple present and simple past tenses

Verbs are action words. They also show when an action took place. The forms that verbs take to show the time of an action is called **tense**.

Read these sentences.

Superheroes **eat** lots of healing superfoods.

I **mixed** everything together to make the potion.

The verb *eat* is in the simple present tense. It tells us something which is always true. It is used for talking about everyday actions and routines.

The verb *mixed* is in the simple past tense. It tells us about an action which happened in the past.

To change a verb to the past tense, we often add -*ed* to it. (*mix* ➔ *mixed*)
Some verbs change form completely. (*send* ➔ *sent*)

Look at the present and past tense forms of these verbs.

Present	Past
learn	learned
dance	danced
cry	cried

Present	Past
go	went
listen	listened
drink	drank

A. Now, complete the table as shown.

	Simple Present Tense	Simple Past Tense
1.	They dance in the rain.	They danced in the rain.
2.		The baby cried loudly.
3.	Sunita reads a storybook at night.	
4.		We painted the walls blue.
5.	I go to my grandmother's house every day.	
6.		I listened to the rain.

usage of *do, does*

We use *do/does* when we want to ask *yes/no* questions.

Do you want to play badminton?

Does your friend sing?

We use *does* with singular nouns and singular pronouns (he, she, it).

Shivum **does** not want to eat.

The sun **does** not rise in the west.

Does *he/she* want to go outside?

We use *do* with plural nouns and pronouns (you, we, they) and with *I* and *you*.

Shivum and his father **do** not want to eat outside.

You/We/They **do** not want to eat outside.

B. Complete the sentences using *do* or *does*.

1. __________ you know Polly?
2. We __________ not have any fruit.
3. Priya __________ not have anything to eat.
4. This question __________ not require much time.
5. What __________ you want to have for breakfast, Riya?

usage of *has, have, had*

Has is used with singular nouns and singular pronouns (he, she, it).

The washing machine **has** *leaked*.

She **has** *bought* an umbrella.

Have is used with plural nouns and with *I, you, we,* and *they*.

They **have** *finished* their work.

I **have** *got* a new notebook.

We **have** not *done* our work.

Had is the past tense of *have* and *has*.

I **had** *completed* the work before it started raining.

When *has, have,* and *had* come before the main verb in a sentence, they are called **helping verbs.**

C. Complete the sentences using *has, have,* or *had*.

1. Peter __________ not come to school today. His parents __________ called the doctor home to check him. His friends __________ decided to make a 'Get well soon' card for him in school today.
2. Mummy, Papa, and I __________ visited grandma before my school opened. Papa __________ prepared breakfast for all of us before we left. Mummy realised she __________ left the car key at home. She went back and took it. I __________ fallen asleep before we reached grandma's house.

Study Skills

Spelling

words with *ll*

Look at these words with the letters *ll* from the story.

In it was a spoonful of **yellow** gooey liquid speckled with tiny black bits.

I added a **dollop** of raw honey.

Let us look at a few more examples: **chill**, **really**, **hall**, **roll**, **shell**

Find and circle at least seven words with *ll* in the word grid.

21ST CENTURY Critical Thinking

S	M	I	I	H	G	P	P
H	J	E	I	I	Y	I	O
A	S	J	O	L	A	L	L
L	B	F	R	L	R	L	L
L	I	L	L	C	T	C	E
O	H	S	M	A	L	L	N
W	J	O	L	L	Y	G	O

Listening

listening to a recipe and sequencing

Listen to the steps for making a sandwich. Then, read the following sentences and number them in the sequence of steps of the recipe.

- ☐ Sprinkle a spoonful of grated cheese.
- ☐ Squeeze some tomato ketchup.
- ☐ Now, put the slices on a dry surface.
- ☐ Place the ready sandwiches on a dry plate.
- ☐ Cover the slice with the other slice and press it lightly.
- ☐ Prepare a *paneer* mixture.
- ☐ Repeat the steps with the other slices.
- ☐ Your delicious snack is ready.
- ☐ Take four slices of bread.
- ☐ Apply butter on the slices.
- ☐ Take the paneer mixture on the slice and spread it evenly.

Speaking

speaking on a given topic

Imagine you were absent from school and you missed out on all the work and fun. Talk to your classmates about how you felt when you did not come to school.

You can include the following points:

- why you were absent
- how you felt when you thought of school, your friends, and your teachers
- how to thank those who helped you with the missed work
- how you feel back in school

Writing

writing a process

Read this description of the process of making a cup of tea.

1. First, boil some fresh water in a saucepan or a kettle.
2. Put a teabag in a cup.
3. Add the boiled water.
4. Leave to brew for 2–3 minutes.
5. Remove the teabag.
6. Add milk and sugar to taste.
7. Stir with a teaspoon.
8. Your cup of tea is ready.

Follow the example to write the process for any one of these.

1. baking a cupcake
2. painting a scenery

Explore More

Read the picture book *Breakfasts of India* (2019). It has information about morning meals from 14 states across the country.

Watch the film *Charlie and the Chocolate Factory*. Charlie is from a poor family. He wins a tour of the grand chocolate factory with other children. Watch the film to know what happens there.

poem

4 Litterbug

Ray Mather

Curricular Goals

- develop a comprehensive range of vocabulary in various contexts
- develop the ability to express themselves in writing

Competencies

- can identify the synonyms and antonyms of words
- can make a collage and write a paragraph

Reading

a *We take care to keep our homes clean, but what about our roads, gardens, parks, and railway stations? Is it not our duty to keep these places clean too? There are many who think it is their right to throw litter on the streets. Read this poem about one such person.*

SUSTAINABLE DEVELOPMENT GOALS 6 CLEAN WATER AND SANITATION

I'm a **litterbug** and I don't care,
I throw my litter everywhere.
Crisp packets, sweet wrappers, lollipop sticks –
In desks, on the yard – the usual **tricks**.

I'm not **bothered** where my rubbish goes;
Let it be carried where the wind blows.
Playing-field, garden – it's no **sin** –
Couldn't care less about the litter bin.

I **trash** the playgrounds and dirty the parks,
Stuff cans in **hedges** – them sort of larks[1].
The street is my **empire**; it swims in **debris**;
It looks ugly to you, but it's lovely to me.

Where did I come from? What is my game[2]?
Me, the person you all like to blame?
What do I look like? Well, I'll have to be true –
I'm not a monster – I'm YOU, YOU and YOU.

Common idioms and proverbs

1. **for a lark:** When we do something for a lark, we do it just for fun though it could be something naughty or dangerous.
2. **What is your game?:** This idiom is used when we want to know what someone's real plans are.

litterbug: someone who drops litter in public places
tricks: (here) naughty or bad things someone does
bothered: worried
sin: something very wrong that you do
couldn't care less: to be not worried
(to) trash: (here) to make dirty
stuff (something): to push something quickly or carelessly into a small space
cans: metal containers of food or soft drinks
hedges: rows of bushes
empire: a very large kingdom
debris: rubbish

In a Nutshell

Who A person who chooses to litter

Where In the parks, gardens, playgrounds, streets, and hedges all around

What The person talks about how fun it is to throw things here and there instead of putting them in the dustbins.

About the poet

Ray Mather (b. 1950) was an English teacher before becoming a writer. He started writing poems for his students. Many of his poems are about school life. Some of his famous poems are 'Remember Me' and 'If I Had a Dog.'

Understanding the Poem

ia **A. Choose the correct options to complete the sentences.**

1. The litterbug throws ______________________________.
   a. sweet wrappers, lollipop sticks, crisp packets
   b. milk bottles, chocolate wrappers, lollipop sticks
   c. sweet wrappers, ice-cream sticks, crisp packets
2. The litterbug stuffs empty cans of food and soft drinks into ____________.
   a. shrubs b. hedges c. trees
3. The litterbug's empire is the ____________.
   a. pavement b. street c. garden
4. The litterbug is ____________.
   a. all of us b. some of us c. one of us

B. Read the lines and answer the questions.

1. *I'm a litterbug and I don't care,*
   I throw my litter everywhere.
   a. Who is the 'I' in these lines?
   b. What kind of a person is he/she? Write two words to describe the person.
   c. Name three things that make up the litter.
2. *The street is my empire; it swims in debris;*
   It looks ugly to you, but it's lovely to me.
   a. Why is the street an empire for the speaker?
   b. What is the meaning of the phrase 'swims in debris'?
   c. Pick out the pair of opposites in the last line.

Life Skills and Values

importance of cleanliness

21ST CENTURY Critical Thinking

1. Why has the poet named the poem 'Litterbug'? What do you think the poet wants to say?
2. Pick out the line in the poem where the 'I' becomes 'you'. What do you think the poet is telling us by making this change?

Vocabulary

synonyms

In the poem, you came across words like **litter**, **rubbish**, **trash**, and **debris** which mean the same thing. They are different names for waste lying around on the streets.

A. Draw lines to match words from the poem that have the same meaning as the given words.

empire — true — bug

1. kingdom
2. honest
3. beautiful
4. typical
5. insect
6. worried

lovely — usual — bothered

antonyms

Look at this line from the poem.

It looks **ugly** to you, but it's **lovely** to me.

The words *ugly* and *lovely* are opposite in meaning and are called **antonyms**.

ia **B. Fill in the blanks with the antonyms of the underlined words. Choose from the words given in the box.**

old	weak	empty	clean	careless

1. The blue can is full, but the red can is __________.
2. Akhil is a strong boy, but his brother is __________.
3. The litterbug makes the park dirty. We should keep it __________.
4. My uncle bought a new truck and is going to sell his __________ one.
5. We must be careful about our surroundings and not be __________ about it.

Activity

making a collage

A. Paste or draw pictures to make a collage on the city or town that you live in.

You can follow these steps to make the collage:

1. Take small craft sheets and draw pictures of places that you would like to see clean. You can paste pictures of parks, monuments, or streets.
2. You could also click photographs or cut out pictures from a magazine.
3. Paste these on a colourful chart paper to make an interesting pattern. You can use sketch pens and coloured sticky tape to add an interesting border.
4. Add an idea box in the corner.
5. Give a caption to your collage.

writing a paragraph

B. Write a paragraph on how we can work together to keep our world clean. Also, write a set of rules that people need to follow to maintain cleanliness.

Explore More

Read the poem *Messy Room* by Shel Silverstein. It describes a child's messy room and has a funny surprise ending.

Watch the film *WALL-E*. It is the story about a robot who lands on Earth in 2805 and tries to clean it up.

Listen to the song *Don't Be a Litterbug*. It teaches children about the importance of not littering and taking care of the environment.

play

5 The Porridge Pincher

David Wood

Curricular Goals

- develop a comprehensive range of vocabulary in various contexts
- develop fluency in reading and the ability to read with comprehension
- sustain effective communication skills for day-to-day interactions
- develop the ability to express themselves in writing

Competencies

- can identify words with two meanings, and use quantifiers and modals correctly
- can sort words in alphabetical order
- can do a role play and write how you feel about it

Reading

a *Three bears went out for a walk in the morning. A little girl, Goldilocks, skipping around in the forest, is drawn to the smell of their breakfast porridge. She enters their cottage and goes through the things in their home. Read the play to find out what happens when the bears return home.*

Characters

Storyteller **Father Bear** **Mother Bear** **Baby Bear** **Goldilocks**

(Enter the Storyteller.)

Storyteller: Down in a country, deep, in a **wood**, is a cottage where once an oak tree stood. Living inside is a family:

(Enter the Three Bears.)

Father: Father!

Mother Bear: Mother!

Baby Bear: And Baby, that's me!

Storyteller: Nobody goes there **unawares**. For this is the home of …

Bears: Three brown bears!

Mother Bear: Time to get up!

Storyteller: Cries Mother one morning.

wood: a large area of trees growing near each other

unawares: unexpectedly

Mother Bear: Rise and Shine[1], Baby Bear, stop yawning! Daddy's cooking breakfast.

Father Bear: Eggs or toast?

Storyteller: Baby Bear thinks,

Baby Bear: What I **fancy** most is porridge, Daddy, porridge please.

Mother Bear: Mmm, sounds tasty,

Storyteller: Mum agrees. So using all his cooking skills, Father heats and stirs and fills three steaming bowls, but then, guess what? They taste it and …

Bears: It's far too hot!

Father Bear: Never mind[2],

Storyteller: Smiles dad.

Father Bear: Don't **fret**, don't **frown**. We'll go for a walk till the porridge cools down. *(Exit The Three Bears. Enter Goldilocks.)*

Storyteller: So, into the woods the bears **withdraw** forgetting to close the cottage door. Now quite by chance and with no **warning** someone else is out this sunny morning, a little girl called Goldilocks in a stripey dress and spotty socks.

As she skips through the wood she suddenly **spies** …

Goldilocks: Gosh, I don't believe my eyes! A cottage! And it looks so **cosy**!

Storyteller: Now Goldilocks is rather **nosy**.

Goldilocks: I must just have a little peep.

Storyteller: So up the path she starts to **creep**.

Goldilocks: Who lives here?

Storyteller: Thinks Goldilocks, but when she goes to give three knocks, she finds …

Goldilocks: The door is open wide. Why don't I take a look inside? Hello! Good morning!

Storyteller: Goldilocks cries,

Goldilocks: Is anyone at home?

Common idioms and phrases

1. **Rise and shine:** This idiom is used to order somebody to get out of bed and be active.
2. **Never mind:** This idiom is used to tell somebody not to worry or be upset.

Who prepared breakfast in the Bear family?

How did Goldilocks enter the cottage?

fancy: want to have something or do something
fret: to worry
frown: to bring the eyebrows closer together when annoyed or worried
withdraw: (here) to leave from somewhere
warning: something written or said about a danger or a problem that might happen
spies: (here) sees something
cosy: comfortable and warm
nosy: too interested in other people's things
creep: to move quietly and slowly

Storyteller: No one replies. She tiptoes in, as softly as she's able and sees the bowls of porridge sitting on the table.

Goldilocks: I must have a little sniff. Mmm, that smells good, I wonder if …

Storyteller: Now Goldilocks was rather greedy.

Goldilocks: I could **scoff** it if I'm speedy! Here's a spoon! Ooo I'm so lucky! Big bowl first! Ugh, that tastes yucky! Much too salty for me to eat. Middle-sized bowl! Ugh, that's too sweet!

Storyteller: The one bowl left is very small,

Goldilocks: But it tastes just right!

Storyteller: So she eats it all! Now Goldilocks fancies a little rest, there are three chairs to choose from.

Goldilocks: Which is best?

Storyteller: She sits on the big one and gets a shock …

Goldilocks: It's **wobbly** and **knobbly** and hard as a rock!

What's hard as a rock?

Storyteller: Next the middle-sized chair by the **telly**, but …

Goldilocks: Oh! It's **squidgy** and soft as jelly!

Storyteller: She spies a small chair …

Goldilocks: This will do!

Storyteller: But Goldilocks is heavy and it breaks in two.

Goldilocks: What have I done? I'd better run!

Storyteller: But she sees a staircase.

Goldilocks: That looks fun! Where does it lead to?

scoff: (here) eat something quickly
wobbly: shaky from side to side
knobbly: uneven due to lumps
telly: short for television
squidgy: soft and can be pressed or crushed easily

Storyteller: Up she heads and finds a room with three brass beds. What happens now isn't hard to guess … She decides to test their **comfiness**. She tries the biggest of the lot.

Goldilocks: This blanket makes me much too hot!

Storyteller: The middle-sized bed feels cool enough,

Goldilocks: But its itchy blanket feels too rough! This little bed is just my size.

Storyteller: She snuggles down and shuts her eyes. Soon she's in the Land of Nod[3]. The Bears come back.

(Enter the Three Bears.)

Father Bear: That's very odd.

Storyteller: Says Father Bear.

Father Bear: For I'm quite sure when we went out, I shut the door.

Mother Bear: Never mind,

Storyteller: Says Mum,

Mother Bear: Let's eat. Come to the table, take a seat.

Father Bear: My porridge!

Storyteller: Growls Dad,

Father Bear: Someone's eaten some!

Mother Bear: And somebody's tasted mine!

Storyteller: Cries Mum.

Baby Bear: And mine as well!

Storyteller: Sobs Baby Bear,

Baby Bear: My bowl is empty! It's not fair!

Common idioms and proverbs

3. **Land of Nod:** This idiom means an imaginary land of sleep.

Did Father Bear close the door?

comfiness: the feeling of being comfortable

Storyteller: Worried by this porridge news the family look around for **clues**.

Father Bear: My cushion's moved!

Storyteller: Growls Father Bear.

Father Bear: Who's been sitting on my chair?

Mother Bear: My cushion's moved and what is more,

Storyteller: Cries Mother Bear,

Mother Bear: It's on the floor!

Baby Bear: Whoever sat upon my chair was much too big,

Storyteller: Cries Baby Bear.

Baby Bear: And look Dad, look Mum, it's no joke, it looks as though they've gone and broke it!

(The Three Bears rush up the stairs.)

Storyteller: Really worried now, the Bears hurry up the wooden stairs. Three heads peep round the bedroom door, then Father Bear is heard to roar,

Father Bear: Who's been sleeping in my bed? There's a **dent** in the pillow from someone's head!

Mother Bear: Who's been …

Storyteller: Growls Mum

Mother Bear: … in my bed asleep and thrown my blankets in a heap?

clues: things that help to solve problems or puzzles   dent: an empty space inside a surface

Storyteller: Baby Bear gets the biggest shock, he sees … guess what?

Baby Bear: A spotty sock! Who's been sleeping in – wait a minute! In my bed – and she's still in it!

Storyteller: His startled **squeal** wakes Goldilocks who jumps up just like a **Jack-in-the-Box**. She opens her eyes and sees the Bears who growl and chase her down the stairs. She **dashes** through the Bears' front door faster than ever she's run before, down the path and through the wood and now she's gone, the Bears say …

Bears: Good!

Storyteller: She's had a very nasty fright. Some would say.

Bears: It serves her right[4]!

Common idioms and proverbs

4. **serves her right:** This idiom means treating someone as they deserve.

Storyteller: The story makes the national news with television interviews. When Goldilocks is asked to say what lesson she learnt that sunny day, she answers …

(Enter Goldilocks.)

Goldilocks: Next time I have found a house I'd like to look around, however much I feel excited I won't go in till I'm invited.

Where did the news appear?

Storyteller: The Bears are asked to **comment** too. They say …

Bears: From now on what we'll do when we go out, is make quite sure we don't forget to lock the door.

squeal: a screaming sound

Jack-in-the-Box: a child's toy with a doll inside a box, which jumps out when the lid is opened

dashes: runs or goes somewhere quickly and suddenly

comment: to give an opinion or explain something

In a Nutshell

Who Goldilocks and the three Bears

Where In the Bears' cottage

What The Bears leave for a walk leaving the front door open. Goldilocks enters without invitation. The Bears return and find Goldilocks using their things.

About the author

David Wood (b. 1944) is an English actor, author, composer, director, magician, and producer. He writes stories and plays for children. His most famous books are *The Gingerbread Man* and *The Phantom Cat of the Opera*, among others.

Comprehension

A. When Goldilocks enters the Bears' cottage, she does many things with their belongings. Fill in the table with what she does, in your notebook. One has been done for you.

	Porridge	Chairs	Beds
Father Bear	She sniffs it. She tastes it.		
Mother Bear			
Baby Bear			

B. Answer these questions.

1. Why did the three Bears go out into the woods?
2. How could Goldilocks enter the cottage?
3. What was Goldilocks doing when the Bears returned home?
4. How did each of the Bears feel when they saw what had happened in their home?
5. What was Goldilocks' reaction when she woke up and saw the Bears?

Life Skills and Values

being curious or being careful

21ST CENTURY Critical Thinking

1. What happened when the Bears found Goldilocks in their house? What lesson did they all learn?
2. Have you ever done anything out of curiosity? Are you always very careful?

Vocabulary

one word, two meanings

Fill in the blanks in each pair of sentences with the given words from the story. You may have to change the form of some of the words.

dear   lost   cook   promise   fit   turn

1. Papa Bear cooked porridge for breakfast. (verb)
   My father is an excellent cook. (noun)
2. The little girl ________________ her way in the forest. (verb)
   The police found the ________________ bag. (adjective)
3. Soni is a ________________ friend of mine. (adjective)
   Hello ________________, how was your day at school? (noun)
4. These new shoes don't ________________ me. (verb)
   Is Rahul ________________ enough to play now? (adjective)
5. The spinning wheel ________________ round and round. (verb)
   Ronita, it's your ________________ to collect the copies today. (noun)
6. Rajni ________________ to help her friend with her craft project. (verb) Please do not break your ________________. (noun)

Grammar

usage of *some, a lot of, any, a few, many, much*

Words like *some, a lot of, any, a few, many,* and *much* are used to refer to the amount or quantity of something.

Examples: **a lot of** money, **many** birds, **much** time

ia **A. Fill in the blanks with the correct options.**

1. I have ______________ (many, much) friends in Mumbai.
2. There are ______________ (many, much) books on the table.
3. Let us buy ______________ (some, many) apples on the way back.
4. These plants can grow without ______________ (much, a few) water.
5. ______________ (A lot of, Much) people were standing at the bus stop.
6. Hurry, there are only ______________ (a few, a lot of) chocolates left on the table!

Read these sentences.

Baby Bear **could** not eat the porridge because it was too hot.

'I **should** not enter anyone's house unless I am invited,' Goldilocks says.

In these sentences, *could* and *should* are examples of words that are used to express ability and intention, respectively.

Uses of more such words are:

- They tell us whether someone has the ability to do something or not. (He **can** dance very well but he **cannot** sing.)
- They tell us whether something will happen or not. (It **may/might** rain tomorrow.)
- They are used for asking permission. (**May** I come in?)
- They are used for making requests. (**May** I take the pencil, please?)
- They are used for giving advice. (You **should** drink plenty of water.)
- They are used for offering something. (**Would** you like to eat an apple?)
- They tell us that something is necessary to be done. (You **must** wash the fruits before eating them.)

ia **B. Fill in the blanks with the correct options.**

1. I ____________ (can/may) paint but I cannot swim.
2. Shobha ____________ (must/might) practise well for the test.
3. Rani ____________ (could/could not) take the train as she was late.
4. Father Bear ____________ (could/should) lock the door when they all go out.
5. You ____________ (should not/cannot) read in dim light as it will harm your eyes.
6. 'You ____________ (must not/could not) wake up the dragon while crossing the mountain,' the magician warned him.

Study Skills

Dictionary Skills

alphabetical order

In a dictionary, words are arranged in the order of the letters of the alphabet. The word *ant* comes before *bark*.

When the first letter of two words are the same, then they are arranged in the order of the second letters, and so on.

So, *battery* comes before *beach*, and *chair* comes before *clever*.

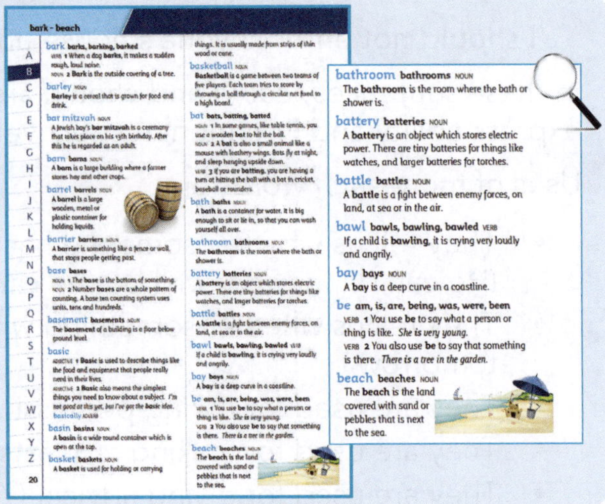

Arrange these words in alphabetical order.

flapping	defeat	entire	chew	messenger
trunk	apart	village	fool	cry
growl	snuggle	wobbly	knobbly	terrible

Listening

listening to a description and drawing

Listen to the passage and draw a picture in your notebook. What is your final picture. Give it a title. Then, write two sentences about your picture.

Speaking

role play: interview

Collaboration
Communication

A. Enact the play in class.

B. Now, pair up in two groups. One group will play the role of an interviewer and the other group as Goldilocks.

The interviewer will ask Goldilocks five questions like these:

- What happened that day in the woods?
- Why did you enter the Bears' cottage?
- Whom did you see at the cottage?
- How did you feel when the Bears found you in their room?
- What did you learn from your experience?

Next, change the roles to interviewer and the Bears. The interviewer can ask five questions about the Bears' day.

Writing

Write a few sentences on how you feel about the role play of the interview. Use the format given below.

How I Feel About the Role Play

I first played the role of ______________________________.

I felt ______________________________

______________________________.

I learnt ______________________________

______________________________.

Then, I played the role of ______________________________.

I felt ______________________________

______________________________.

I learnt ______________________________

______________________________.

Explore More

Read the story *Charlotte's Web* by E.B. White. Charlotte is a spider who tries to save her friend Wilbur, by writing messages on her web.

Watch the film *Charlotte's Web* based on the book by E.B. White.

Project 1

A. Work in groups of four. Read about the solar system. Collect your information. Now, make a poster on your favourite part of the solar system.

It can be any planet, the moon, or the sun.

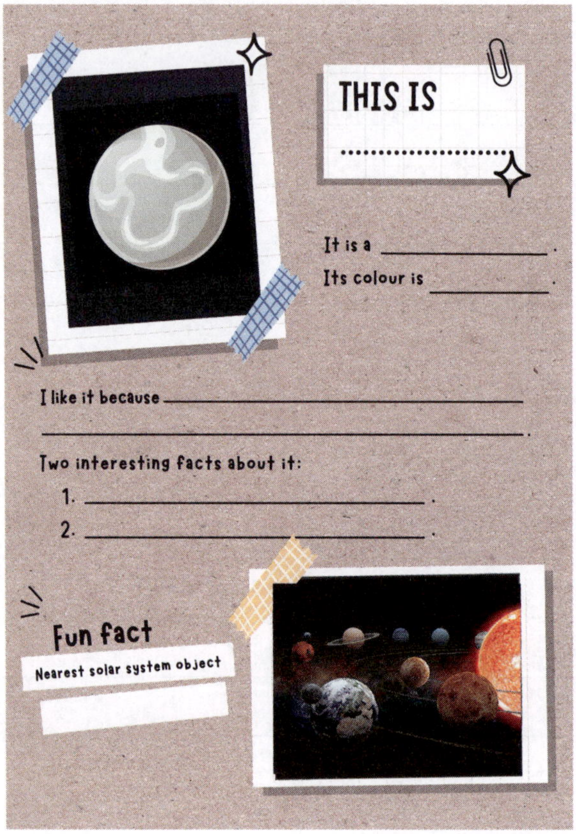

B. Have you ever seen a mural?

A mural is a picture painted on a wall. Look at these murals. All these murals are from different palaces in Rajasthan. Rajasthan is known for its murals.

You read about the importance of cleanliness in 'Litterbug'. Now, design a mural for your school to create awareness about cleanliness. Add a slogan to your mural. Talk about it in class.

UNIT

III

Nature Around Us

Critical Thinking

Warm-up

A. Who am I? Solve these riddles about insects and match them.

1. I am as busy as can be. I make honey for you and me.
   I buzz as I fly. Who am I?
2. I hop across the grass. I have long back legs.
   Who am I?
3. I am round and red with black spots all over. I am a little lady!
   Who am I?
4. I am colourful and beautiful. I fly among flowers and plants.
   Children love me. Who am I?

B. Have you ever seen a windmill? What makes it work? Let us make a paper pinwheel that looks like a windmill.

Materials required: a square piece of paper, a pin, and a long paper cup.

1 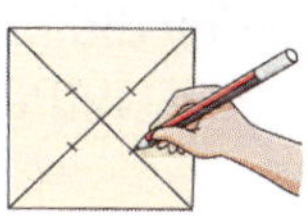

Step 1. Take a sheet of paper. Fold the paper square twice, corner to corner, and then unfold. Make a pencil mark about 1/3 of the way from the centre.

2 

Step 2. Cut along the fold lines. Stop at your pencil mark.

3 

Step 3. Bring all the points into the centre and stick a pin through all four points.

4 

Step 4. Roll the pin around in small circles to make the hole bigger. This will help your pinwheel to spin freely.

5 

Step 5. Turn your paper cup upside down and stick the pinwheel on the side.

Your windmill is ready to turn with the wind!

short story

6 A Butterfly Smile

Mathangi Subramanian

Curricular Goals

- develop a comprehensive range of vocabulary in various contexts
- develop fluency in reading and the ability to read with comprehension
- sustain effective communication skills for day-to-day interactions
- develop the ability to express themselves in writing

→

Competencies

- can understand similes, movement words, different functions of adjectives, and comparison of adjectives
- can use reflexive pronouns and form plurals
- can introduce themselves and write an informal letter

Reading

a *Where have you seen butterflies the most, in your garden or somewhere else? Can you guess how the butterfly helps to protect the environment? Read the story to find out more.*

'Line up, class! Let's go to the park,' Laila Miss called out.

The children held hands as they **chattered** away.

Kavya stood by herself.

As they started to walk, Laila Miss asked, 'Does anyone know what a caterpillar becomes when it grows up?'

Kavya's heart jumped. She knew the answer! Should she speak up?

> Why did Kavya's heart jump?

Kavya and her family had just moved to Bengaluru from their village.

They lived at the **construction site** where her parents worked. It was hard living in a half-finished house. The air smelt of smoke, and the **honking** traffic made it hard to sleep. The **towering** buildings, **zooming** cars, and busy people made her feel small and afraid.

Kavya had been going to school for a week. She still hadn't spoken to anyone. What if they made fun of her **accent** or teased her because she had never been to school before?

Kavya took a deep breath and raised her hand. In a noisy city like Bengaluru, she couldn't be quiet forever! Besides, Laila Miss had a kind smile.

chattered: spoke about unimportant matters
construction site: place where a building is being built
honking: (here) loud
towering: very high
zooming: very fast
accent: a way of speaking a language that shows the country or region someone comes from

'When a caterpillar grows up, it becomes a butterfly,' Kavya said.

'That's right!' Laila Miss smiled.

'Caterpillars are only caterpillars for a few weeks,' Kavya said. 'They spend their whole time eating leaves.'

'They must get very big,' said Mary, her classmate.

'Yes, they do!'

How long do caterpillars stay inside cocoons before they change their form?

'After they eat and eat and eat, caterpillars become bigger and bigger. When they grow big enough, they find a place on the sides of plants and weave a **cocoon** around themselves,' said Kavya.

'That's correct,' Laila Miss said. 'They stay in their cocoons for a few weeks and slowly change their form. When they come out, they are butterflies.'

'Look, we're at the park!' Mary cried out.

Kavya **gasped**. The park was full of butterflies!

Blue butterflies—the colour of rivers.

Yellow butterflies—the colour of sunlight.

Orange butterflies—the colour of ripe apricots.

Black-and-white butterflies—the colours of starry skies.

Cross-curricular Corner

Monarch butterflies are known to travel over 3,200 km from Canada to Mexico during autumn.

These were the colours Kavya missed from her village. She felt her heart **flutter**.

'Every year, many butterflies travel thousands of kilometres to come to this park. They come here for more food, better weather and a safe place to lay eggs,' Laila Miss said. 'This journey is called **migration**.'

'Don't they get tired, **flapping** their wings for so long?' a classmate asked.

What is migration?

cocoon: a cover of silky threads made by young insects to rest in while they change into an adult
gasped: breathed quickly and noisily in surprise
flutter: (here) to beat quickly
migration: the movement of animals or birds from one place to another
flapping: moving up and down

'If there is a strong wind, they don't have to flap their wings,' Kavya said. 'They just spread their wings and **glide**.'

'That must be **bumpy**,' Mary whispered to Kavya.

Kavya thought about the bus ride to Bengaluru–squeezed in between all the luggage–bumping and **tumbling** for hours and hours.

Is that how a butterfly felt in the wind?

'When butterflies migrate, they follow rivers. To stay healthy, they stop along the riverbank to soak up minerals with their feet. It's called mud-puddling,' Laila Miss said.

'Mud-puddling?' Mary said. 'That sounds like fun.'

Mary and Kavya smiled at each other.

'It is,' Kavya said. 'But now puddles are hard to find.'

In Kavya's village, men in trucks took sand away from the river. The weather became hotter and hotter every year. There was less and less rain. Last year, the river went dry.

The butterflies didn't have enough water to mud-puddle and Kavya's family didn't have enough water to farm. That's why they moved to Bengaluru.

'You know a lot about butterflies, Kavya,' said Laila Miss.

'That's because they are my favourite insects,' said Kavya.

'Why do you love butterflies so much, Kavya?' asked Mary.

For the first time that day, Kavya did not know the answer. There was so much to love. How could she pick just one reason?

Common idioms and proverbs

butterflies in my stomach: This idiom means we are feeling very nervous. It describes the fluttering feeling we get in our stomach.

Why did Laila Miss praise Kavya?

glide: move smoothly
bumpy: (of a journey) uncomfortable with a lot of sudden movements
tumbling: falling suddenly

Butterflies were beautiful. Some were covered in spots, others in stripes. She loved to watch them drink **nectar** with their long tube-like mouths. They were friends of flowers. They spread **pollen**, which made more flowers and fruits grow.

'They fly far, but wherever they land, they make new friends,' Kavya said, smiling at Mary. 'They're very small, but they're also very brave.'

'Just like you,' Laila Miss said.

Kavya smiled a smile as wide as a butterfly's wings[1].

Literary term

1. This is a **simile**. Here, Kavya's smile is being compared to a butterfly's wings. It tells us how wide her smile was.

nectar: a sweet liquid that flowers make which birds and insects drink

pollen: a fine powder produced by flowers which help produce new seeds

In a Nutshell

Who Kavya, a shy and quiet girl

Where In a new school in Bengaluru

What She enjoyed a field trip to the park where she saw many butterflies.

About the author

Mathangi Subramanian is an author and educator. She believes stories have the power to change the world. She has won many awards for her books and short stories.

Comprehension

ia **A. Number these sentences in the order of events in the story.**

- ☐ Kavya's class went to a park.
- ☐ Kavya's parents worked at a construction site.
- ☐ The big city made Kavya feel small and afraid.
- ☐ The teacher asked them about butterflies.
- ☐ Kavya did not speak to anyone for a week at her new school.
- ☐ Kavya and her family had moved to Bengaluru.
- ☐ Kavya knew a lot about butterflies.
- ☐ The teacher was very pleased with Kavya.

B. Answer these questions.

1. Why did Kavya's parents move to the city?
2. What did Kavya see in the park?
3. What is mud-puddling?
4. Why did Kavya love butterflies?
5. Why do butterflies migrate?

Life Skills and Values

overcoming difficulties and showing empathy

21ST CENTURY Critical Thinking

1. Do you think Kavya was a shy girl? Give reasons for your answer.
2. What kind of difficulties did Kavya's family face? Mention any two.
3. There is a new student in your class. How will you introduce yourself? What will you do to make her comfortable?

Vocabulary

similes

In the story, you came across the words 'a smile as wide as a butterfly's wings'. When two persons or things are compared using 'as' or 'like', it is called a **simile**.

ia **A. Choose the correct word to complete the simile in each sentence.**

1. Brr! My hands are as cold as ____________ (juice/ice).
2. The village looks as pretty as a ____________ (picture/cartoon).
3. There you are! I can see you are as busy as a ____________ (bee/wasp).
4. Is there some food? I am as hungry as a ____________ (horse/butterfly).
5. Little Rani is well-mannered. She is as good as ____________ (silver/gold).
6. Where are your books? The bag is as light as a ____________ (paper/feather).

words related to movement

Words that show movement are called **movement words**.

Read these sentences.

The *heart* **flutters**.

The *wings* **flap**.

The *wings* **spread out**.

The *butterflies* **fly**.

The words *flutters, flap, spread out,* and *fly* show movement of the nouns.

B. Fill in the blanks with movement words from the story. You may have to change the word to match the correct tense.

fluttered	flap	glide	jump	fly	zoom

1. The fox __jumped__ over the fence.
2. The eagles ______________ very high.
3. The chicks ______________ their tiny wings.
4. The ships ______________ across the silent sea.
5. The motor bikes ______________ across the race track.
6. The butterflies ______________ their wings in the breeze.

Grammar

functions of adjectives

Read this sentence from the story.

They drink nectar with their **long** tube-like mouths.

The word *long* tells us something about the noun *mouths*. It is an adjective.

Adjectives are words which describe nouns or pronouns and give us more information about them.

Adjectives are used in the following ways:

Adjectives

Adjectives can tell us about the size, shape, and quality of a noun.

Examples: In a **noisy** city like Bengaluru, she couldn't be **quiet** forever!

Rani wants the **small** bottle and the **square** pencil box.

They can also tell us about how many or how much of something there is.

Examples: Kavya saw **seven** butterflies.

I put **some** salt in the soup.

ia A. Fill in the blanks with the correct adjectives.

gentle   red   some   favourite   fast   safe

1. The rabbit is a ________________ animal.
2. It is not ________________ to climb hills at night.
3. *Alice in Wonderland* is my ________________ book.
4. We need to add ________________ salt in the salad.
5. Please take the ________________ train to reach on time.
6. The parrot has green feathers and a ________________ beak.

comparison of adjectives

Read these sentences.

Kavya was **quieter** than the other children in her new school.

In Kavya's village, the weather became **warmer** every year.

If the wind is not strong, butterflies have to flap their wings for a **longer** time.

When we compare two things, we add -*er* to the describing word.

quiet → quiet**er**

warm → warm**er**

long → long**er**

Language Booster

An adjective in the comparative form is always followed by *than*.

Example: A cat is smaller *than* a tiger.

ia B. Fill in the blanks by adding -*er* to the words given in brackets.

1. She is ________________ (smart) than her brother.
2. The sea is ________________ (deep) than the river.
3. The frock is ________________ (long) than the shirt.
4. The chocolate is ________________ (sweet) than the cake.
5. The handbag is ________________ (light) than the suitcase.

Read these sentences.

Kavya spoke up for **herself**.

The caterpillar weaves a cocoon around **itself**.

The words *herself* and *itself* are pronouns. We use these pronouns to talk about the main naming word in a sentence. Here are more such pronouns.

I – *myself*	you – *yourself*
he – *himself*	she – *herself*
it – *itself*	we – *ourselves*
they – *themselves*	

ia **C. Fill in the blanks with the correct pronouns.**

1. She made ________________ a cup of tea.
2. We enjoyed ________________ at the party.
3. They were talking amongst ________________.
4. My dog is always scratching ________________.
5. Avyaan fell from his bicycle and hurt ________________.

Study Skills

Spelling

forming plurals

1. You know that we form plurals by adding -*s* to nouns.
   Examples: books, girls, boys
   cats, schools
2. When the noun ends in *s, sh, ch, o,* and *x,* then we add -*es.*
   Examples: bus → buses bush → bushes
   torch → torches mango → mangoes
   box → boxes
3. When a noun ends in *f* or *fe,* we change the *f* or *fe* to -*ves.*
   Examples: leaf → leaves knife → knives
   loaf → loaves wife → wives
4. When a noun ends with *y,* we drop the *y* and add -*ies.*
   Examples: baby → babies fry → fries
   body → bodies

Some of the following plural nouns have incorrect spellings. Circle the incorrect spellings. Then, write them correctly.

1. wifes ____________
2. tomatoes ____________
3. volcanos ____________
4. knifes ____________
5. cries ____________
6. jellys ____________
7. punches ____________
8. foxs ____________
9. fruites ____________
10. roses ____________

Listening

listening to a poem and gap filling

Listen to a poem about a caterpillar and fill in the blanks.

1. The caterpillar in the poem is brown and ____________.
2. We know that it is moving quickly because the poet says that it is in a ____________.
3. The caterpillar is searching for a shady ____________ or ____________ to rest in.
4. The caterpillar has to hide itself from the ____________.
5. Another danger lies in the birds of ____________ who are hovering above.
6. It will lastly turn into a ____________.

Dictation

Listen to a passage about a butterfly and write it down. Each sentence will be repeated twice.

Speaking

role play: introducing yourself

Read about Kavya introducing herself in class. Imagine that you have joined a new school, like Kavya. Introduce yourself to the class. Include the following points in your introduction:

- your name and age
- where you are from
- special hobbies or things you enjoy
- a special achievement

Writing

writing an informal letter

Imagine that you are Kavya. Write a letter to your cousin Priyanka telling her about your experience of the field trip to the park.

Points to include in your letter:

- why you felt shy about speaking up in class
- what made you change your mind
- what you told the class about butterflies
- your friendship with Mary and how you feel about school now

You may use the given format.

C-23 Rajajinagara
Bengaluru - 560010 — Sender's address

Date ______________ — Date

Greeting — Dear Priyanka,

How have you been? I have so much to share with you. Did you know that we have moved to Bengaluru? It is such a big city. Here, . . . ______________________________
____
______________________________ — Body

Do give my regards to uncle and aunty and love to little Mishu. I can't wait to hear from you.

Yours lovingly, — Closing phrase
Sender's name — Kavya

Explore More

Read the story *Pollyanna*. It is about a young girl called Pollyanna. She comes to a new place, tries to adjust to her new life, and spreads hope.

Watch the film *A Bug's Life*. An ant tries to save his colony from greedy grasshoppers with the help of other insects.

7 poem

The Wind

Paul King

Curricular Goals

- develop a comprehensive range of vocabulary in various contexts
- develop the ability to express themselves in writing

Competencies

- can identify and use sound words in sentences
- can describe a picture

Reading

a *Have you ever flown a kite on a windy day or tried to put pegs on clothes hung out to dry? Has the wind ever blown your papers or umbrella away? Read a poem about the playful wind.*

The wind is a fellow to **sport** and to play,
He'll **billow** and **bellow** and **bluster** all day,
He's up from the hillside and over the **lea**,
He's airy, **contrary**, and quick as can be.

'No one can catch me!' he boasts with a shout,
But in the **mill sails** his mistake he'll find out!
Just **harness** him there and he'll give you his power
To **grind** all your **harvested wheatgrain** to flour.

Cross-curricular Corner

A windmill uses the power of the wind to crush grain or make electricity. It does so with the help of sails.

sport: (here) to play with
billow: fill out with air and move slowly in the wind
bellow: shout angrily
bluster: blow noisily, show off
lea: an open area of grassy land, a meadow
contrary: in a way that people think is wrong or naughty

mill sails: sails on a windmill
harness: to control something for a useful purpose
grind: to crush
harvested: (of crops) gathered
wheatgrain: grains of wheat

In a Nutshell

Who The wind

What It is like an active and lively little boy.

Where In the countryside

About the poet

Paul King wrote poems for his students while working as a teacher in South Africa and Ireland. Presently, he lives in England, after his retirement.

Understanding the Poem

A. Choose the correct options.

1. In the poem, what is the wind like?
   a. It is like a lively animal. ☐
   b. It is like a mischievous friend to play with. ☐
   c. It is like a game. ☐
2. Where does the wind blow in the poem?
   a. It blows across trees and rooftops. ☐
   b. It blows across rivers and seas. ☐
   c. It blows across the hills and meadows. ☐
3. Why does the wind think he cannot be caught?
   a. He thinks he is too quick to be caught. ☐
   b. He thinks he is too clever to be caught. ☐
   c. He thinks he is invisible and cannot be caught. ☐
4. What power does the wind have?
   a. He has the power to run the machines in the mill. ☐
   b. He has the power to blow things away. ☐
   c. He has the power to destroy the earth. ☐

B. Read the lines and answer the questions.

1. *He'll billow and bellow and bluster all day*
   a. Who is 'he' in the above line?
   b. What does 'he' do all day? Mention three actions.
   c. Which word in the line is something people may do when they are angry?
2. *But in the mill sails his mistake he'll find out!*
   a. What will happen in the mill sails?
   b. What mistake has the wind made?
   c. What will the wind help grind in the mill?

Life Skills and Values

knowing your potential

1. Do you think the wind discovers its value when harnessed by the wind sails? What lesson do you learn from it?
2. There may be many things that you feel you can do better or can improve upon. Mention two such things that you can do differently so that you feel happy and satisfied with your effort.

Vocabulary

word grid

A. You read that the wind *billows* and *blusters* as it blows. There are many such sound words related to the noise the wind makes as it blows. Find these words and circle at least five of them in the word grid. Sound words are also called onomatopoeia.

H	U	M	P	Y	M	C	G	J	M	S	J	S	S
S	A	S	P	B	N	N	C	S	I	G	H	U	W
A	K	I	N	L	C	K	R	O	P	I	I	P	O
C	N	V	W	L	J	N	G	U	S	T	H	V	O
Z	A	E	Y	H	O	W	L	Q	S	O	G	Q	S
T	J	N	S	K	O	Y	M	C	N	H	Q	O	H
Q	K	P	W	T	W	O	R	H	S	F	Q	S	B
H	I	E	I	J	B	V	S	M	D	N	N	P	X
I	O	K	S	X	U	O	W	H	I	S	P	E	R
S	P	C	H	C	L	Z	S	J	P	S	Z	N	K
S	G	T	E	T	Y	Z	F	R	B	E	F	Q	C
R	U	S	T	L	E	T	F	I	D	V	F	D	P

making sentences

B. Now, make sentences with any four words you found in the word grid.

1. ______________________
2. ______________________
3. ______________________
4. ______________________

Activity picture composition

Look at the picture. Write a paragraph to describe what you see. Give a suitable title to your description.

____

____

____

____

____

____

____

____

Explore More

Read the poem *The Wind on the Hill* by A.A. Milne. The poem describes a child's wonder at where the wind comes from.

Watch the film *The Boy Who Harnessed the Wind* by Chiwetel Ejiofor. It is a true story about a 13-year-old boy who builds a wind turbine to help his village cope with famine.

UNIT
IV

Humour

Warm-up

A. Are you scared of tigers? Have you ever thought that a tiger could be funny too? Let's enjoy a few tiger jokes.

Why did the tiger lose at cards?
Because he was playing with a cheetah!

What do tigers wear in bed?
Stripey pyjamas!

Now, give funny endings of your own to the following jokes. The jumbled words are there to help you.

What do you call a tiger who copied in his school test?

________________________________ (Hint: CPOYTAC)

How do tigers greet human beings?

________________________________ (Hint: SPELAED OT TEA OYU!)

B. Some people make us laugh more than others. Think of someone who makes you laugh. Then, fill in the word web.

Someone who makes me laugh: ____________________

Something they say: ____________________

Something they do: ____________________

Something they wear or carry: ____________________

short story

8 Drip, Drip

Alka Shankar and Sharleen Mukundan

Curricular Goals

- develop a comprehensive range of vocabulary in various contexts
- develop fluency in reading and the ability to read with comprehension
- sustain effective communication skills for day-to-day interactions
- develop the ability to express themselves in writing

Competencies

- can understand homophones and word pairs, identify plural, possessive, and collective nouns, and use prepositions
- can narrate a story and write a paragraph in the past tense

Reading

a *Have you read of great heroes and warriors who fought bravely for their king or country? What would happen if someone became a hero by accident? Find out in this story.*

A tiger was caught in a storm one evening—he had **wandered** into the fields looking for something to eat. He **huddled** close to the wall of Naini's hut for shelter. Naini was an **ill-tempered** old woman who lived on the outskirts of the village. She was feeling especially ill-tempered that day, because her roof was leaking badly.

'This drip-drip!' she **muttered**, pushing her tin **trunks** and bed from place to place to keep them dry. 'Is there no escape?' She **slammed** the bed against a trunk, picked up a small wooden box, and **shoved** it against the wall. The wall shook.

The tiger felt the wall shake and heard Naini shout, 'It's killing me, this drip-drip!'

The tiger was puzzled and frightened. 'What could this drip-drip be? It makes such a terrible noise. It must be a **dreadful** creature!'

Just then Bholenath, the potter, passed by. He was in a bad mood, too. His donkey had run away. He suddenly saw an animal huddled against the wall of a hut. 'There he is!' he shouted and running to the tiger, kicked it. Then he pulled the tiger's ears. 'Move, or I'll break your bones!'

wandered: walked around
huddled: sat with arms and legs close to its body
ill-tempered: very angry and annoyed
muttered: spoke quietly, murmured
trunks: large, strong boxes for storing things
slammed: (here) banged something against something else, making a loud noise
shoved: pushed
dreadful: terrible, very bad

The tiger was really frightened. 'This must be that terrible Drip-Drip,' he thought. Without a growl, he followed the potter home. When they reached Bholenath's hut, the potter tied the tiger outside with a strong rope. 'You can stay out in the rain!' he shouted.

What did Bholenath mistake the tiger for?

The potter's wife got up early the next morning. As she came out of the hut, she saw the tiger and screamed. Bholenath came running out. He **stopped short** when he saw the tiger. Then he turned and ran. His wife followed him, still screaming. They shut the door of their hut and pushed their bed and trunks against it.

Other people in the village were awake by now. They saw the **snarling** tiger tied outside Bholenath's hut. **Astonished**, they hurried off to tell others about it.

Why were the villagers astonished?

The **terrified** tiger finally chewed through the rope, and ran back to the jungle.

After a while Bholenath peeped through a small hole in the door. 'The tiger's gone!' he whispered. Trembling but **relieved**, he opened the door.

Many people came to visit Bholenath that day. 'Did you really kick him? asked the carpenter.

Bholenath had recovered from his fright now. 'I not only kicked and slapped him, I even pulled his ears,' he replied with a laugh.

Word of the incident spread until even the king heard the story. He sent for the potter and said, 'I have never heard of such bravery! We need men like you in the army.

You shall be my General!'

One evening, when the whole court was gathered, a soldier rushed in crying, 'War!

The neighbouring king has **declared** war. He's at our borders with eighty thousand men!'

The king called Bholenath, 'The time has come to prove your bravery. I **appoint** you my Commander-in-Chief.'

'I-I will do my best,' Bholenath stammered, his heart beating loudly with fear.

That night Bholenath said in **despair** to his wife, 'I don't even know how to ride a horse. What will I do?'

stopped short: stopped suddenly
snarling: growling angrily
astonished: surprised
terrified: scared
relieved: happy that something bad has stopped happening
declared: announced
appoint: choose somebody for some work
despair: hopelessness

'Don't worry,' she replied. 'I'll tie you to the horse. What happens after that is in God's hands.'

Early the next morning, a messenger arrived with a handsome black **stallion**. 'It belongs to the king himself! He has sent it for you to ride into **battle**.'

Bholenath unhappily followed his wife out to the horse. Four servants lifted him onto the black stallion, then his wife tied him **securely** to the horse. She even tied one end of the rope to the horse's tail. The horse didn't like the feel of all these ropes, and **rearing up** suddenly, galloped off with Bholenath holding on **desperately**. Suddenly, Bholenath realised that the horse was heading straight for the enemy camp.

Why was Bholenath holding on desperately?

'No, no!' the potter shouted. He saw a banyan tree with its **aerial roots** hanging over the road. As the horse galloped under it, Bholenath reached up to pull himself free. But the horse was going too fast and the roots came right off the branches, and hung flapping in his hands.

'Help! Help!' the potter shouted, waving the roots to attract attention.

The horse galloped straight into the enemy camp. The soldiers saw a wild-looking man, hair and clothes flapping, ropes all around him, on a fierce black stallion, waving tree roots and shouting.

'It's the advance guard!' a soldier yelled. 'It's a **demon**!' screamed another. 'The king has a demon army!' shouted a third. 'Run!' cried a fourth. 'Run!' echoed the others and ran for their lives.

Cross-curricular Corner

The **advance guard** is a group of soldiers who go first and prepare the way for the main army.

Bholenath's horse reached the middle of the camp. The ropes that had tied the potter to the horse came undone and he fell off the horse. He looked around the empty camp **bewildered**. Then, slowly and painfully, he stood up and led the horse back home.

The king's army had ridden out to join their Commander. They met him walking **wearily** home.

'The enemy has gone,' he told them.

stallion: a male horse
battle: a fight between enemy forces
securely: tightly
rearing up: (here) raising the front legs up
desperately: fearfully
aerial roots: roots that grow from the stem of a plant
demon: an evil spirit
bewildered: surprised
wearily: in a very tired way

The soldiers rode to the camp to see for themselves. The camp was empty. The soldiers rode **triumphantly** into the city and told the king what had happened.

> Why was the king delighted?

'Scared away a whole army single-handed?' cried the king delightedly. 'What a man!'

Even today, people tell the story of the brave potter who caught a tiger and **defeated** an entire army all by himself.

triumphantly: proudly, having won over the enemy

defeated: won over somebody in a battle, game, or contest

In a Nutshell

Who Bholenath, the potter in the village

What He became a hero.

How By defeating the enemy by mistake

About the authors

Alka Shankar is famous for her children's books. Her well-known book is *The Mighty and the Mystical Rivers of India*. Sharleen Mukundan is a famous children's writer. She has written *Murthy: The Storybook* with Alka Shankar.

Comprehension

ia **A. Choose the correct options.**

1. Who took shelter behind Naini's hut?
   a. a tiger   b. a donkey   c. a stray animal
2. What was Drip-Drip?
   a. the sound of Naini kicking the trunks
   b. the sound of the wall of the cottage shaking
   c. the sound of water falling from the leaking roof
3. Why did Bholenath become the King's Commander-in-Chief?
   a. because the news of him catching the tiger spread everywhere
   b. because the villagers told the King how brave Bholenath was
   c. because he told the king how he kicked and slapped the tiger and pulled his ears

4. Why was Bholenath able to drive away the enemy?
    a. because he was extremely brave
    b. because the enemy got frightened seeing his wild appearance and loud shouting
    c. because he was a demon on a wild horse

B. Read the lines and answer the questions.

1. *This must be that terrible Drip-Drip!*
    a. Who said these words and to whom?
    b. What was 'Drip-Drip'?
    c. Why does the speaker think it was terrible?
2. *I have never heard of such bravery!*
    a. Who said these words and to whom?
    b. What bravery was the speaker talking about?
    c. What role did the speaker give to the brave person?

Life Skills and Values

appreciating humour and heroism

21ST CENTURY Critical Thinking

1. Did you find the story funny? Pick out two incidents that made you laugh.
2. Did anyone come forward to help the potter? Why/why not?
3. Was Bholenath a real hero? Give reasons for your answer.

Vocabulary

homophones

Some words sound the same but have different spellings and meanings. They are called **homophones.**

Examples: son – sun, beet – beat, flower – flour

ia **A. Fill in the blanks with the correct options.**

1. The monkey has a long ____________ (tail/tale).
2. The ____________ (bear/bare) lives in the jungle.
3. ____________ (Pore/Pour) the milk into the glass.
4. I felt a sharp ____________ (pane/pain) in my ankle.
5. Please take a ____________ (write/right) turn to reach my house.
6. The painting is available for ____________ (sail/sale) until Saturday.

Some words are used in pairs. They are joined with *and*, *or*, and *by* to make different word pairs. The words in these word pairs are always used in the same order. For instance, you always say, 'bread and butter', not 'butter and bread'.

Examples: loud and clear, right or wrong, step by step

B. Complete the word pairs in these sentences.

white   tidy   quiet   later   sound   little

1. Please keep your room **neat and** ____________.
2. There was **peace and** ____________ in the library.
3. We saved enough money, **little by** ____________, to buy a house.
4. After the rains stopped, we got back home **safe and** ____________.
5. When my parents were young, they only had **black and** ____________ TVs.
6. You will have to do the work **sooner or** ____________, so why not do it now?

Grammar

nouns: plural and possessive

We know that plural nouns give the names of more than one person, place, or thing. We usually show this by adding -*s* to nouns.

Examples: trunks, roots, soldiers

Nouns can also show that something belongs to somebody. We do this by adding 's to the noun.

Examples: Mary's umbrella, mother's bag

For plural nouns that end in -*s*, we only add the apostrophe (').

Examples: boys' hostel, doctors' chamber, teachers' staffroom

A. Tick the correct sentences. Rewrite the incorrect sentences correctly in your notebook.

1. Ram is absent. This is Ram's seat.
2. Hi! This is Sheena, my sister. That is Sheenas cycle.
3. This is a big shop. Let us look at the childrens toys.

4. That is the boys' hostel. Which way is the girl's hostel?
5. The costumes are ready. These are the dancers' costumes.

collective nouns

A **collective noun** is a noun that refers to a group of people, animals, or things.

Collective nouns are generally considered singular because they are one group. Look at these examples.

An **army** of eighty thousand soldiers has gathered at the border. (*army* of soldiers)

A **herd** of cows is grazing quietly in the field. (*herd* of cows)

The nouns *army* and *herd* are collective nouns.

ia **B. Fill in the blanks with the correct collective nouns.**

1. He carried a ____________ (bunch/bundle) of clothes.
2. We saw a ____________ (team/herd) of cattle in the field.
3. A ____________ (pack/pride) of lions attacked the hunters.
4. She kept a ____________ (collection/bunch) of keys on the table.
5. A large ____________ (colony/crowd) of people gathered in front of our house.
6. She gave her mother a ____________ (bouquet/bundle) of flowers on her birthday.

prepositions of position and time

Read these sentences.

The tiger was **outside** the gate.

The potter's wife woke up **in** the morning.

The words *outside* and *in* are examples of **prepositions**. *Outside* is preposition of position and *in* is preposition of time in these sentences.

Prepositions show the relation between a noun or a pronoun and other words in a sentence. They give information about position and time.

Here are some common prepositions: *in, on, at, under, near, over, from, between, before, with, to, beside, across, during*

ia **C. Fill in the blanks with the correct prepositions.**

1. The river flows ____________ (under/across) the bridge.
2. The basket of mangoes is ____________ (on/in) the table.
3. The child sat ____________ (beside/between) her mother.
4. The bank closes at 3:00 p.m. ____________ (at/in) the afternoon.
5. The spring season begins ____________ (in/on) the month of March.
6. School reopens after the summer holidays ____________ (on/in) 1st July.

Study Skills

Pronunciation

sounds of homophones

As you have already seen, **homophones** are words that sound the same.

Fill in the blanks with the correct homophones. Then, say them aloud.

1. Get up, ____________. It is morning. (son/sun)
2. The ____________ has a short bushy tail. (hair/hare)
3. Nobody will be able to ____________ what I share ____________. (hear/here)
4. She ____________ along the ____________ covered with flowers. (road/rode)
5. The children played for ____________ hours. That is ____________ long. They need ____________ eat and then sleep soon. (too/two/to)

Listening

listening to a passage and gap filling

Listen to a story. Then, complete the sentences using words from the story.

1. The tailor killed seven ____________ with one blow.
2. The tailor made himself a ____________ to let the world know of his bravery.
3. The tailor carried a piece of ____________ and a little ____________ in his pocket.
4. In the mountains, the tailor met a ____________.
5. The giant squeezed water from a ____________.
6. The tailor squeezed water out of his ____________.
7. The giant threw a ____________ high up in the air.
8. The clever tailor threw up the little bird, which ____________.

Speaking

narrating a story with picture clues

Creativity

Now, look at these pictures and tell the story of the clever tailor in your own words.

Writing

writing in the past tense

Creativity

Imagine that you are the tiger in the story. Describe what happened to you in a paragraph.

You may begin this way:

One day, I was caught in a storm …

Useful words and phrases

walked around – hungry – hut as a shelter – walls shook – woman talking – Drip-Drip – puzzled and confused – terrible noise – demon – kicked – pulled my ears – followed him out of fright – tied outside all night – man and woman – screamed and ran away – people staring – chewed through the rope

Explore More

Read the story *The Tiger Who Came to Tea* by Judith Kerr. It is about a tiger who joins Sophie and her mother for tea one afternoon.

Watch the film *Kung Fu Panda*. Po, a lazy panda, tries to save the Valley from an enemy.

9 poem

The Green Hedgehog

Celia Warren

Curricular Goals

- develop a comprehensive range of vocabulary in various contexts
- develop the ability to express themselves in writing

Competencies

- can understand collocations and homographs
- can write a funny poem

Reading

a *The poet is writing about a young boy and his pet. The boy was worried as the pet was not moving and it looked pale. He took it to the vets who said that they could not treat it. Read this humorous poem to find out why.*

I had a little hedgehog.
It was green and looked quite ill.
Its **spines** were thin and **pale**
And it sat completely still.
Its eyes were closed so tightly,
I knew it couldn't see.
It seemed to have just lumps and bumps
Where its feet should be.
I took my hedgehog to the vets,
Afraid it might be dead;
The vets took one look at it
And this is what they said:
'This sad and sorry **article**
Has nothing to **attract** us.
I'm sorry to inform you
That your hedgehog is
… a cactus!'

spines: long sharp points on an animal's body or on a plant
pale: washed out, colourless as in ill
article: any object or thing
attract: to draw interest or attention to any thing

In a Nutshell

What The boy found out something about his pet.

When He took it to the vet.

Why It appeared ill and he wanted to find out what was wrong.

About the poet

Celia Warren has been writing poetry for children for a long time. She has compiled two anthologies, *The RSPB Anthology of Wildlife Poems* and *A Time to Speak and a Time to Listen*. Her latest book is *Don't Poke a Worm Till It Wriggles*.

Understanding the Poem

A. Answer these questions.

1. What is the poem about?
2. What was the colour of the boy's pet?
3. Where did the boy take his pet?
4. What did the boy think had happened to his pet?
5. What did the boy think the pet was?
6. What was the boy's pet in reality?

ia **B. State whether the following sentences are true (T) or false (F).**

1. The boy's pet was an animal. ☐
2. The boy was worried about his pet. ☐
3. The pet had lumps and bumps where its feet should have been. ☐
4. The boy did not know what his pet was. ☐
5. The vets treated his pet. ☐

Life Skills and Values

taking care of others

21ST CENTURY Critical Thinking

1. The vet told the boy that his hedgehog was a cactus. How do you think he felt? How would you feel if you were in place of the boy?
2. Do you help when someone you know and care about feels unwell or sad? How do you feel after helping them?

Vocabulary

collocations

We often use two or more words together because they go together.

Examples: harsh winter (not *strict winter*)   heavy snowfall (not *thick snowfall*)

A. Fill in the blanks with the correct options.

1. Mother Teresa had a kind ______________ (mind, heart, life).
2. There were ______________ (heavy, thick, fast) rains last night.
3. A cucumber sandwich is a ______________ (fit, healthy, fast) snack.
4. Fast ______________ (food, water, burger) is not good for your health.
5. There is a ______________ (bright, light, shining) sun shining in the sky this morning!

homographs

Homographs are words that are spelled the same but have different meanings.

Sometimes the words are pronounced differently too.

Be careful of the cactus **spines**. (long, sharp points on an animal's body or on a plant)

Our **spine** is made of 33 bones. (the row of bones down your back)

Place the books on the shelf with the **spine** showing clearly. (the narrow stiff part of a book which the pages and covers are attached to)

The word *spine(s)* is spelled the same in all three sentences but with different meanings.

B. Fill in the blanks with the correct homographs given in the box.

rose	fly	close

1. Birds ______________ high in the sky.
2. A ______________ almost fell into my soup.
3. ______________ the door when you leave.
4. You are standing too ______________ to the edge of the pavement.
5. The ______________ has soft velvety petals.
6. Grandma ______________ from her chair to fetch her glasses.

Note: The homographs in this exercise are different in meaning but have the same sound/pronunciation.

Activity

pictogram

We sometimes use pictures to say what we mean. Some examples of these are road signs and signs at the airport.

A. Try to guess the meanings of any four signs and write them down in your notebook.

writing a funny poem

B. You may have a pet, a favourite stuffed toy, a book, or a 'comfort' article that you hold onto and take it everywhere you go. You feel so much love for it that it feels like a real person you care about.

1. Do you have a 'comfort' toy/pet/book/plant/anything else? What is it?

   ____

2. Write two things that make you feel attached to it.

   ____

   ____

Now, write a funny poem about your pet or article and make a drawing of it in your notebook.

Explore More

Read the book *Stop Snoring, Bernard!* By Zachariah OHora. Bernard the otter loves curling up to go to sleep. But he snores loudly. He keeps all awake during naptime. Read the story to find out what happens then.

Watch the film *Fly Away Home*. Amy stumbles upon a collection of abandoned goose eggs. When the eggs hatch, Amy and her dad work together to teach the birds to fly south for the winter.

Listen to the song *Do You Want to Build a Snowman* from the film *Frozen*.

Answers to Self-Assessment given on page 9

A.	1. night	2. found	3. short	4. dirty
B.	a. boxes	b. plates	c. matches	d. brushes
	e. bottles	f. tomatoes		
C.	1. tall	2. deep	3. wide	4. heavy
	5. strong			
D.	1. under	2. at	3. between	4. on
	5. in	6. over		
E.	1. We/our	2. I/my	3. He/his	4. You/your
F.	1. is resting	2. slipped, fell	3. was eating	4. is running
	5. was writing	6. is sitting, like	7. started, goes	

Project 2

A. You read about butterflies in 'A Butterfly Smile'. Now, create a booklet on butterflies. Form groups of six and look up the Internet to collect information on any six butterflies. Present your information as shown. Include pictures or drawings. Give a name to your booklet.

Butterfly 1

Name: Tiger Swallowtail butterfly

Where it is found: woods and river valleys of North America.

Description: Light yellow with dark stripes like those of a tiger.

Butterfly 2

Name: Monarch butterfly

Where it is found: North America, Central America, India, Western Europe

Description: Reddish yellow with dark stripes and markings. The wings have a dark border with white spots.

B. Fun is as important as studying. Form teams of six. Then, follow the given steps to play a game.

monkey drool spider pancake milk banana peel

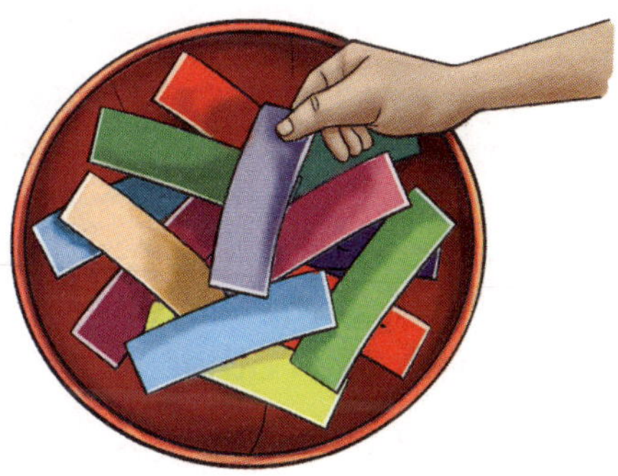

Step 1: Write the given action words on separate strips of paper. You can add more words if you want.

Step 2: Fold the strips and place them in a bowl.

Step 3: One member from a team will pick a strip.

Step 4: The team member will act out the action and the other team members will guess the word.

Step 5: Ensure every team and every team member gets a chance to act.

Get, Set, Play!

UNIT V

Friends and Family

Warm-up

A family is a group of people who are related to each other. Do you know what a family tree is? It is a chart which shows the relationship between the members of a family.

A. Make a family tree like the one given below. Write a unique quality for each member.

Example: grandmother (mother's mother) – good at crosswords

Many families who live in a place make up a community. People in a community are similar in some ways and usually know each other. Sometimes, they become friends with each other.

B. What are the things people in a community do for each other? List three people from your community and write one thing that they do to help you. Follow the example given.

People	What they do for us
1. Rama aunty, our neighbour	She looks after our plants when we are on holiday.

graphic story

10 Paplu, the Giant

Ramendra Kumar

Curricular Goals

- develop a comprehensive range of vocabulary in various contexts
- develop fluency in reading and the ability to read with comprehension
- sustain effective communication skills for day-to-day interactions
- develop the ability to express themselves in writing

→

Competencies

- can use sound words and different conjunctions, identify the subject and predicate in a sentence, and say the hard and soft sounds of *g*
- can do a role play and make a poster

Reading

a *Giants are imaginary creatures who roamed the earth a long, long time ago. They were usually shown as being huge in size, and angry and cruel in nature. Read this story about a nine-year-old giant called Paplu, who was different.*

A young boy called Paplu lived in a village with his mother. Paplu was a giant, but he was not like other giants at all. Giants love to fight, but Paplu hated fighting.

Paplu's mother was worried about her son. One night, she took him to a village where human beings lived. Before entering the village, she **shrank** herself and Paplu to one-tenth their size.

Paplu liked living with Raghav. He made friends with the children in the village. One day, Raghav came home very worried.

Paplu's mother had taught him the magic words for becoming a giant again. He tried everything he could to remember them, like standing on his head, and pulling his own ears.

shrank: became smaller
tribe: a group of people usually of the same community who live and work together
bandit: an armed robber
starve: to die from not having any food to eat
defeat: to beat or make your enemy lose

froze: suddenly stopped and became still

swelling up: becoming bigger

chant: group of words spoken over and over again

(in your) birthday suit: not wearing any clothes

'**Operation** Paplu Dress' started.

In seven hours, the clothes were ready. Paplu stood up, **towering over** the villagers.

Just after midnight, Paplu set out to meet Angaar and his men. The bandits heard a strange sound and rushed out of their tents. A dust storm had begun. Trees swayed and lightning **crackled**.

The strong wind lifted Angaar up. It flung his **deputy Jarnail** and his best **swordsman**, Talwar, into the air too. A few minutes later, there was a splash.

The men landed in the river near the village. As they swam to the shore, **spluttering** and **shivering**, they saw a huge shadow over their heads. Who was it?

operation: important activity involving many people
towering over: standing taller and higher than others
crackled: made sharp loud noises
deputy: someone in the second highest position
swordsman: someone who fights with a sword
spluttering: spitting out water noisily
shivering: shaking because of the cold
roughed up: beaten up

Cross-curricular Corner

The name **Jarnail** comes from the word **General**, which means a senior officer in the army, navy, or air force.

Similarly, the name **Talwar** comes from the Hindi word for sword.

Paplu went back to the village. Angaar and his men left the same night and were never heard of again. Paplu went back to his original shape and size. But from then on, to everyone, and even to Soni, he was Paplu, the Giant.

In a Nutshell

Who Paplu, the 9-year-old giant

Where In a human village near a river

What He helped save the villagers from bandits.

How Paplu could become a giant and return to human size with the help of magic.

About the author

Ramendra Kumar is an award-winning Indian writer who has written 35 books in English for children and adults. *A Tale of Tails*, *A Tsunami Called Naani*, *We Are Different*, and *A Perfect Match* are some of his well-known books. His work has been translated into many regional languages.

Comprehension

A. Complete the flow chart to show the order of events in the story. Fill in the blanks with words or phrases.

1. Paplu was a giant but he hated fighting. So his mother shrank him and took him to a ____________, where he started living with ____________ beings.
2. Angaar, the bandit, had blocked the ____________ the village. Raghav was worried that the villagers would ____________.
3. Paplu wanted to help the villagers but he had forgotten the ____________ his mother had taught him to become big again.
4. A ____________ girl helped him to remember the magic words. Paplu threw up a ____________ and said the magic words.
5. He became a giant again but one without any ____________. So, all the ____________ of the village got together and made a set of clothes for ____________.
6. Paplu wore the ____________ and he beat up ____________ and saved the villagers. He became the guardian of the ____________.

B. Read the lines and answer the questions.

1. *Son, you will never be happy in our tribe.*
   a. Who said these words and to whom?
   b. Why did the speaker think her son would not be happy there?
   c. Where did she take her son?
2. *But Maharaj, please tell me, who are you? I have never seen you in these parts.*
   a. Who said these words?
   b. Why did he address Paplu as 'Maharaj'?
   c. What happened to the speaker at the end of the story?

Life Skills and Values

being different

Critical Thinking

1. Use five adjectives to describe Paplu.
2. How was Paplu different from his tribe and from the people in the village?
3. How did that difference affect his life? How did it make him feel about himself?

Vocabulary

contextual usage

A. Fill in the blanks with words and phrases from the story.

shrank   roughed up   take care of   gang   froze   from then on

1. ____________________, Arun never missed a game.
2. When I saw the tiger, I ____________________ in fright.
3. There is a nurse to ____________________ the old man.
4. Alice ____________________ herself to pass through the tiny door in the wall.
5. The police caught the ____________________ of thieves after the theft at the bank.
6. The burglars ____________________ the shopkeeper until he handed over all the money.

sound words

There are many words that sound like the action they refer to. These are called **sound words**.

Examples: There was a loud **splash** as the boy jumped into the pool.
Big drops of rain **plopped** on the ground.

ia B. Fill in the blanks with the correct options.

crash   chatter   drip drip   jingle   slurp

1. He drank his milk with a noisy ____________ .
2. I could hear the ____________ of water all night.
3. The bowls fell on the floor with a loud ____________ .
4. I was thrilled to hear the ____________ of Christmas bells.
5. There was an excited ____________ of voices coming from the playground.

Grammar

subject and predicate

Every sentence has a **subject** and a **predicate**.

The **subject** tells us who or what the sentence is about. The **predicate** tells us something about the subject. It has a verb in it.

Examples: **Paplu** was a giant.

The bandits heard a strange sound.

In the first sentence, *Paplu* is the **subject**, and *was a giant* is the **predicate**.

In the second sentence, *The bandits* is the **subject**, and *heard a strange sound* is the **predicate**.

Language Booster

In a sentence, predicate is everything else other than the subject.

A. Read the sentences. Underline the subjects and circle the predicates.

1. The peacock has beautiful feathers.
2. The villagers were afraid of the tiger.
3. My mother carries an umbrella every day.
4. Arun Singh has written a beautiful story for children.
5. All the children reached the planetarium before 10 a.m.
6. I finished my homework before my mother cooked dinner.

B. Fill in the table to complete the sentences.

	Subject	Predicate
1.	Anita and Soham	
2.		is having breakfast.
3.		are relaxing in the garden.
4.	My pet kitten	
5.		plays the piano.
6.	They	

conjunctions *and, but, so, or*

Conjunctions are joining words. They join words and sentences.

Examples: Giants love to fight, **but** Paplu hated fighting.

Some common conjunctions are *and, but, or,* and *so.*

Examples: Do you want to have Indian food **or** Chinese food?

I have to study, **so** I won't be able to play now.

Language Booster

We use *and* to add similar words or sentences.

Example: I have a cap and a hat.

We use *but* to show difference.

Example: I like to dance but my sister likes to sing.

We use *or* to show choice.

Example: Do you want an apple or a banana?

C. Fill in the blanks with the correct conjunctions from the box.

and	or	so	but

1. I have porridge _______________ fruits for breakfast.
2. Would you like to have butter _______________ jam?
3. Sunil is good at cricket _______________ not at football.
4. Both my father _______________ my mother go to office every day.
5. There were no vegetables at home, _______________ we went to buy them.

Study Skills

Pronunciation

hard and soft sounds of *g*

The letter *g* makes two sounds: hard and soft. Read out loud these sets of words.

Hard *g*	Soft *g*
game	gem
gold	giraffe

When *g* comes before *a, o,* or *u,* its sound is hard: *garden, goblin, gum.*

When *g* comes before *e, i,* or *y,* its sound is usually soft: *gentle, gypsy, ginger, large.* (Not for *gift!*)

Say these words aloud and put them in the correct columns.

1. gum
2. gym
3. huge
4. tragedy
5. gang
6. goose
7. giraffe
8. gift

g as in 'gold'	*g* as in 'gem'

Listening

listening to a passage and stating true or false

Listen to a passage about a giant and state whether these sentences are true (T) or false (F).

1. There were beautiful flowers in the garden. ☐
2. The peach trees bore pink, white, and green flowers. ☐
3. In winter, the trees bore fruit. ☐
4. The children were very happy in the garden. ☐
5. The children did not pay attention to the singing of the birds. ☐
6. The giant had stayed with his friend for five years. ☐
7. He got very angry when he saw the children playing in his garden. ☐
8. The giant would not allow anyone to play in his garden. ☐

Dictation

Listen to a few sentences and write them down. Be careful and spell the words correctly.

Speaking

role play: asking for and offering help

A. Work in pairs. Enact the following conversation.

Raja: Hello, Maya. May I ask you for a favour?

Maya: Hello, Raja. Yes, you can.

Raja: Could you please return this book for me at the library? I am late for football practice.

Maya: Yes, of course. I will return it along with my own books.

Raja: Thank you so much!

Maya: You are welcome.

B. Now, enact the following situations with your partner.

1. Ask your friend if you can borrow a pencil as yours is broken.
2. Ask your elder brother if he could help you with your homework.

Writing

making a poster

Make a poster announcing a reward for catching the bandit, Angaar.

WANTED

Name: ____________________

Description: ____________________

Crime: ____________________

Reward: ____________________

If found, please call ____________

Steps:

1. Draw a picture or paste an image of the bandit.
2. Write the name of the wanted person and mention the crime.
3. Write about the reward offered.
4. Write the name and contact details of the person giving the reward.
5. Draw a border around your poster.

Explore More

Read the story *The Giving Tree* by Shel Silverstein. It is about a tree selflessly helping a boy as he grows up.

Watch the film *The BFG* based on Roald Dahl's story. It is an adventure of Sophie and her friend who is a giant.

graphic story 11

Brown Bear and Wilbur Wolf

Sarah Parry

Curricular Goals

- develop a comprehensive range of vocabulary in various contexts
- develop fluency in reading and the ability to read with comprehension
- sustain effective communication skills for day-to-day interactions
- develop the ability to express themselves in writing

→

Competencies

- can form compound words, add suffixes, and use punctuations
- can understand what adverbs are and make negative sentences
- can complete a dialogue and write a notice

Reading

a *Brown Bear woke up after his winter sleep and felt hungry. He was unable to find food because he had lost his sense of smell. Lonely and hungry, he looked for a friend to talk to. Read the story to see if Brown Bear gets to make a friend.*

Brown Bear was hungry. He'd been asleep all winter. He came out of his den and **stretched**. The snow had melted and the grass was green. Brown Bear looked around him and **sniffed** the air, but he couldn't smell anything.

He went into the forest to look for berries, but he couldn't smell anything.

stretched: put the arms and legs out straight and tightened the muscles

sniffed: breathed in air through the nose

He went to the river to look for fish, but he couldn't smell anything.

'I've lost my smell,' he said sadly to himself. 'How will I find any food?' He lay down in a meadow by the river and tried to remember all his favourite smells – the smell of trees, the smell of new grass, the smell of apples and leaves, of berries, of rain and snow.

'I feel so lonely without my smell,' Brown Bear said. 'Perhaps it wouldn't be so bad if I had a friend to talk to.' But he was all alone.

What happened to Brown Bear's smell?

The birds thought Brown Bear looked sad, so they flew down to play with him.

Brown Bear was pleased to see them and jumped up, but the birds got a fright[1] and flew away.

Why couldn't Brown Bear make friends with the animals?

Common idioms and phrases

1. **take/get (a) fright:** It is a phrase which means being afraid of something and running away.

The beaver saw Brown Bear in the field and thought he looked sad. He called Brown Bear over to his **dam**.

Brown Bear ran towards him, but the beaver got a fright[2] and hid under the branches.

The deer walked into the field and saw Brown Bear looking sad, so they skipped towards him.

Brown Bear stood on his back legs to say hello, but the deer got a fright[2] and turned back.

dam: a wall built across a river or stream to hold back water

Literary term

2. It is an example of **repetition**. The writer uses the same phrase over and over again in a piece of writing, for effect.

Brown Bear lay down. He was all alone and was still hungry.

Wilbur Wolf came out of the forest. He was old and tired and had been looking for food all winter. He saw Brown Bear in the field and walked slowly towards him. 'Maybe Brown Bear can tell me where to find some food,' Wilbur said to himself.

Brown Bear was too tired and hungry to get up when Wilbur came near, so Wilbur wasn't scared. They lay in the tall grass, and Brown Bear explained that he'd lost his smell.

'Without my smell, how will I find any food?' Brown Bear asked.

Wilbur **shrugged**, 'I'm old and weak,' he said. 'How will I catch any food?'

shrugged: raised the shoulders to show disinterest or lack of knowledge

They lay quietly for a while and then Brown Bear said, 'Perhaps we can look for food together. You can be my smell and I'm strong to catch food for us both.'

'We can try,' Wilbur said. And they did. From that day they stayed together – Wilbur would sniff out the berries or the fish and strong Brown Bear would gather enough food for them to share.

So they walked the valleys and mountains, forests and **riverbeds** together and neither ever felt lonely or hungry again.

riverbeds: the ground which a river flows over

In a Nutshell

Who Brown Bear and Wilbur Wolf

What Brown Bear lost his sense of smell. He was hungry and lonely and wanted a friend.

When When he woke up from his winter sleep

How He met Wilbur Wolf. They decided to look for food together.

Cross-curricular Corner

When bears stay asleep all winter, it is called hibernation. It is the way for many animals—from butterflies, bats to bears—to survive the cold and dark winters without having to search for food.

Comprehension

Answer these questions in brief.

1. What did Brown Bear lose when he woke up from his winter sleep?
2. How did Brown Bear feel then?
3. Which animals did Brown Bear try to make friends with?
4. What happened when he went near the other animals?
5. What was Brown Bear doing when Wilbur Wolf went near him?
6. What was Wilbur Wolf looking for?

Life Skills and Values

making and being friends

Critical Thinking

1. How do Brown Bear and Wilbur Wolf help each other and become good friends?
2. Write the qualities that you want in a friend.
3. Write the qualities that make you a good friend.

Vocabulary

compound words

A **compound word** is formed by joining two words.

Examples: river + bed = riverbed   note + book = notebook
lime + stone = limestone

A. Match the words correctly to form compound words.

1. life	a. mint
2. butter	b. fly
3. mile	c. hopper
4. sand	d. storm
5. grass	e. stone
6. pepper	f. time

suffixes

A **suffix** is a group of letters added to the end of a word to make a new word.

Examples:

slow + ly = slow**ly**	child + ish = child**ish**
care + less = care**less**	nation + al = nation**al**
colour + ful = colour**ful**	king + dom = king**dom**
stretch + ed = stretch**ed**	good + ness = good**ness**
punish + ment = punish**ment**	friend + ship = friend**ship**

B. Choose suitable suffixes from the box to make new words. Some words may take more than one suffix.

-er   -ly   -less   -ful   -ment   -ness   -ship   -ish

1. gentle: ________	4. fool: ________	7. direct: ________
2. sad: ________	5. owner: ________	8. tall: ________
3. fear: ________	6. refresh: ________	9. cheer: ________

Grammar

An **adverb** tells us more about a verb.

Adverbs tell us where, when, and how an action takes place.

Examples:

Brown Bear lay **down**.

We are playing **outside**.

I shall go to the market **tomorrow**.

I will go **now**.

Brown Bear and Wilbur Wolf lay **quietly**.

She lifted the baby **gently**.

ia A. Fill in the blanks with adverbs from the box.

carefully	patiently	downstairs	today	outside	recently

1. I want the work to be done today.
2. Oh no, I have left my keys __________!
3. The stranger was standing __________.
4. Rana was waiting __________ in the queue.
5. There was a robbery __________ at the bank.
6. The student answered the question __________.

ia B. Fill in the blanks using adverbs. Form the adverbs by adding *-ly* to the adjectives given in the brackets.

1. The singer is singing ________________ (beautiful).
2. Talk ________________ (soft) as the baby is sleeping.
3. Wilbur Wolf walked ________________ (slow) towards Brown Bear.
4. The king was walking ________________ (proud) among the crowd.
5. The man was lying ________________ (comfortable) under the tree.

Read these sentences.

Brown Bear did **not** have any friend.

Brown Bear was **not** strong enough to find food for himself.

Such sentences with **not** are called **negative sentences**. These are formed by adding *not* to helping verbs.

Examples: is + not am + not are + not
did + not was + not

C. Change the sentences into negative by adding *not*.

1. Soham is studying. ____________________
2. We are going to Delhi. ____________________
3. Children are playing in the park. ____________________
4. The farmer is working in the field. ____________________
5. My mother is baking a cake for me. ____________________

Read this sentence.

Brown Bear had his favourite smells—the smell of trees, apples, berries, rain and snow.

1. All sentences begin with a **capital letter**.
2. The **comma** helps us to separate things in a list and pause at the right places while reading a long sentence.
3. A sentence ends with a **full stop**. Sentences that give information or make requests end with a full stop.

All proper nouns begin with a capital letter. *Brown Bear* is the bear's name, which is a proper noun. So, it begins with a capital letter.

D. Punctuate the following passage using capital letters, commas, and full stop.

mani rohan and sunil went to the market with their aunt jyoti to buy fruits like apple banana and mangoes and some household goods like table mats a tray and spoons on the way they met mr robin smith and his wife mrs maria smith who were also going to the market

Study Skills

Spelling

suffix *-tion*

Suffixes are letters added to the end of words to change their meanings.

Example: inform + *-tion*

inform becomes *information.*

Any word that ends in *-tion* is a noun. It turns a verb into a noun.

If the word ends in *-ne*, *-ve*, or *-re*, it drops the *-e* and adds *-ation.*

Examples: prepare becomes **preparation**.
starve becomes **starvation**.
determine becomes **determination**.

Add *-tion* after the given words to form new words. Note that the spellings change.

	Word		Changed word
1.	protect	ADD suffix *-tion*	
2.	subtract		
3.	suggest		
4.	operate		
5.	relate		
6.	oppose		
7.	react		
8.	introduce		
9.	translate		
10.	admire		

Listening

listening for details

Listen to the passage and answer the questions that follow.

1. How many types of bears are there in the world?
2. What happens when bears come across something new and unfamiliar?
3. What do bears do when they are curious to know about a new sight or sound?
4. Why are bears often misunderstood as attacking?
5. What are mother bears like with their young cubs?

Dictation

Listen to a passage and write it down. Each sentence will be repeated twice.

Speaking

completing a dialogue

Work in pairs. Imagine you are Mani. One evening, you meet Ranu at the park. Complete and enact the following conversation.

Mani: Hello, my name is Mani.

Ranu: Hi. I am Ranu.

Mani: I have seen you here several times, but I didn't know you. So, today I came to talk to you.

Ranu: That's nice. Do you come here regularly or do you stay in this neighbourhood?

Continue the conversation. You can talk about the following:

- your schools
- the games that you like to play
- other interests that you might have
- a suitable ending to the conversation

Writing

writing notices for *Lost* and *Wanted*

Both Brown Bear and Wilbur Wolf need friends who can find food for them. Complete these two notices informing others about what they want.

LOST

I have lost my

____________.

I need a ____________ to help me

____

berries and fish to eat.

Brown Bear

WANTED

I need a good friend to help me

____________________.

I am ____________ and ____________ but I can still sniff out food.

Wilbur Wolf

Explore More

Read the book *Winnie the Pooh* by A.A. Milne. It talks about the adventures of Pooh Bear, Christopher Robin, and his friends.

Watch the film *Brother Bear*. A young hunter turns into a bear after killing a bear. A talkative cub is the only one who can help him change back.

Listen to the song *Bare Necessities* from the film *The Jungle Book*.

short story

12

Heidi Meets Grandfather

Johanna Spyri

Curricular Goals

- develop a comprehensive range of vocabulary in various contexts
- develop fluency in reading and the ability to read with comprehension
- sustain effective communication skills for day-to-day interactions
- develop the ability to express themselves in writing

→

Competencies

- can understand antonyms, collocations, subject–verb agreement, and articles
- can rearrange letters to form meaningful words
- can make a request, thank someone, and describe similarities and dissimilarities in two pictures

Reading

a *Heidi was a young orphan who lived with her aunt, Dete. She was brought to live with her grandfather, whom she met for the first time. He lived in a cottage near the snow-covered Alps. Read the story to know about her first day with her grandfather.*

After aunt Dete left, grandfather sat on his bench again, silent, with his eyes looking down. Heidi saw the goat-shed and peeped in, but saw nothing. Her eyes searched for other interesting things. Behind the hut, she found three old fir trees and as the wind **bellowed**, the trees swayed from side to side. She stood listening to the wind rush through the branches and leaves. Then she returned to grandfather. He was seated exactly as before. She stood firmly in front of him, with her arms behind her back.

'What is it you want?' he asked.

'I want to see inside the hut,' replied Heidi.

'Come then, and bring your things,' he said, as he got up to enter the cottage.

'I do not want them anymore,' answered Heidi. 'I want to be like the **light-footed** goats!'

'All right, but fetch them and we'll put them in the cupboard.' The child obeyed and followed him into a fairly spacious room. A table and a chair in one corner, grandfather's

bellowed: (here) made a roaring sound like an animal   light-footed: moving lightly and quickly bed in another. Across the room was a **hearth** with a large kettle **suspended** over it, and opposite that was a large door in the wall – his cupboard. One shelf had a few shirts, socks, and towels; another had a few plates, cups, and glasses; the top shelf had a loaf of bread, some bacon and cheese... Grandfather kept all in this. After putting her things in deep into the back, she looked around the room and asked, 'Where am I going to sleep, grandfather?'

'Wherever you like,' he replied. Delighted, Heidi began peeping everywhere to find a cosy place to sleep. She climbed the ladder beside grandfather's bed, to reach the **loft**. It was filled with fresh and **fragrant** hay and had a tiny round window, through which she could see the valley below. 'I want to sleep up here,' Heidi called down and adding on, 'I am making the bed now. I need a sheet. Every bed must have a sheet.'

Rummaging through his cupboard, grandfather pulled out a long rough cloth from under his shirts. With it, he climbed up to the loft, where a neat little bed was already prepared, with hay heaped up high at the head of the bed, facing the window.

How did grandfather make Heidi's bed?

They put the heavy sheet on the bed and tucked the ends in. Heidi looked thoughtfully at her fresh, new bed and said, 'We have forgotten something. When I go to bed I always **creep** in between the sheet and the cover.'

Heidi said she could use some hay to cover herself with. Just then, grandfather rushed downstairs and brought a large, heavy linen sack that was kept on his bed.

Heidi pulled the sack with all her might[1], but was unable to unfold it. Then, grandfather put the thick cover on the bed while Heidi watched him. When the bed was complete, she said, 'What a nice bed I have now, and what a **splendid** cover! I wish the evening was here, that I might go to sleep in it.'

Common idioms and phrases

1. **with all one's might:** If you do something with all your might, you do it using all your strength and energy.

Grandfather mentioned food and suddenly she realised how hungry she was. With her excitement about the bed, Heidi had forgotten about food. Before her long journey that morning, she only had a piece of bread and a cup of coffee.

Moving to the fireplace, he pushed the big kettle aside and reached for a smaller one suspended on a chain. Sitting on a three-legged stool next to it, he lit up a bright fire. As the kettle began to boil, grandfather put a large piece of cheese on a long iron fork, and held it over the fire, turning it slowly, till it was golden-brown on all sides.

hearth: the floor of a fireplace, which sometimes extends into the room

suspended: (here) hung

loft: space near the roof of a house

fragrant: pleasant- and sweet-smelling

rummaging: (here) searching for something in a hurried way

creep: to move quietly and slowly

splendid: extremely good

Remembering all that was kept in his cupboard, Heidi ran to it and brought out plates, knives, and bread to set the table. When her grandfather brought a pot and the toasted cheese, everything else was ready and waiting. Looking at the steaming pot, Heidi rushed back to the cupboard and returned with a bowl and two glasses.

Common idioms and phrases

2. **take a deep/long breath:** It is a phrase which means to take a pause after doing something.

Grandfather observed that Heidi's stool was very low and Heidi herself was too little. She wouldn't be able to reach the table. Grandfather filled the little bowl with milk, placed it on his chair, and pushed it towards Heidi's stool. Now Heidi had a little table with a little bowl of milk within reach. After drinking the milk in one go, Heidi took a long breath[2] and set the bowl down.

'How do you like the milk?' grandfather asked her. 'I never tasted better,' she answered.

Grandfather refilled the little bowl; little Heidi ate the bread and cheese and drank the milk with the greatest enjoyment. Once she was done, both promptly went out to the goat-shed. Heidi watched as grandfather moved about, first to put fresh straw for the goats, and then to his little workshop where he began to make a little chair. Realizing that the chair was her size, she was full of **admiration** at how quickly he made it.

Literary term

3. This is an example of **onomatopoeia**. When something dry brushes against something similar, it makes the sound 'rustle'.

Where was the sound of the shrill whistle coming from?

In the evening, while grandfather stood at the door, Heidi played outside the hut, dancing around the old fir trees, as they **rustled**[3] against the mighty wind roaring past them. The sounds filled her heart with happiness. It felt wonderful.

Suddenly a shrill whistle was heard. From higher up on the mountain, came a herd of goats, with Peter walking among them. Joyfully, Heidi ran out to greet the flock. When the herd reached the house, one white and one brown goat stepped out ahead of the rest and walked up to grandfather, who held out his hand to feed them some salt like he did every night.

admiration: a feeling of great liking and respect for someone

rustled: made a soft sound

Heidi used this opportunity to **caress** them, one at a time.

Cross-curricular Corner

Alpine goats are found throughout the Alps mountains. They have great agility to climb the steep mountain slopes.

'Are they ours, grandfather? Do they both belong to us? Are they going to the shed? Are they going to stay with us?' asked Heidi in excitement. Grandfather tried to keep up with her questions. Once the goats were done, grandfather asked Heidi to get her bowl and the bread from inside the hut. With the bowl in hand, grandfather milked the white goat and cut a piece of bread. He told her to eat and then go to bed, while he looked after the goats and locked them up for the night. 'Good night,' he said. 'Good night, grandfather!'

Soon after Heidi had eaten and gone to bed, it got darker and grandfather decided to go to sleep too. He would be waking up early, when the sun came up. The stormy winds still blew through the night, making the hut shake and the boards creak. It howled in the chimney and dry branches of the old fir trees fell around near the hut. Grandfather decided to check on Heidi thinking she might be afraid. It was dark when he climbed up the ladder and reached her bed. In the moonlight that lit up the room, he saw Heidi lay peacefully asleep in her bed, cheeks burning red with a smile on her face. Grandfather waited until the moon hid again behind some clouds, and went down to his bed.

caress: to stroke someone or something gently

In a Nutshell

Who Heidi, a young girl

Where In a cottage near the Alps mountains

When When she came to stay with her grandfather

What She adjusted in her new life.

About the author

Johanna Spyri (1827–1901) was a Swiss writer. Her most famous work is *Heidi*, which is loved by children all over the world. Her love for her homeland and nature can be seen in her writings.

Comprehension

Complete these sentences.

1. Inside his cupboard, Grandfather kept ______________________________.
2. Heidi climbed up to the loft filled with ______________.
3. Heidi made her bed using ______________.
4. Grandfather gave Heidi ______________ to eat and ______________ to drink.
5. When Peter brought the goats home, Grandfather ______________________________.
6. Grandfather climbed up to check on Heidi because ______________.

Life Skills and Values

family, adjusting to a new environment

21ST CENTURY Critical Thinking

1. How was Heidi feeling at the end of her first day with her grandfather? Pick out incidents from the passage that show this.
2. What helped her adjust to the new place and situation?
3. Think of a time when you had to do something new or something you had never done before. How did you feel at that time? How did you deal with the new situation?

Vocabulary

antonyms

Look at these sentences.

He pulled out a **rough** cloth. She wanted a **soft** cloth. (*rough* – *soft*)

Heidi's chair was too **low**. She needed a **high** one. (*low* – *high*)

The words are opposite in meaning. They are called **antonyms**.

ia **A. Write down the antonyms of the underlined words.**

1. It is a <u>cloudy</u> day. ______________
2. Akhil is a <u>strong</u> boy. ______________
3. We took the <u>narrow</u> road. ______________
4. The king was <u>kind</u> to his people. ______________
5. I need help to <u>close</u> this suitcase. ______________

Read these sentences.

Everything else was **ready and waiting**.

A **shrill whistle** was heard.

Stormy winds blew.

The words in blue are pairs of words that are commonly used together.

B. Complete the sentences with the correct words that go together.

homework snow whispered plane regular soap making

1. Mary ____________ softly in my ear.
2. ____________ exercise will help you stay fit.
3. I would like to buy two bars of ____________ please.
4. ____________ was falling as our ____________ took off.
5. I always try to do my ____________ in the morning, after ____________ my bed.

Grammar

subject–verb agreement

Subjects and verbs must agree in number in sentences.

Read the following sentences from the story.

Heidi creeps in between the sheet and the cover. (*Heidi* is a singular subject. It takes a singular verb *creeps*.)

The **goats lick** the salt from Grandfather's hand. (*goats* is a plural subject. It takes a plural verb *lick*.)

A. Circle the verbs that agree with the nouns in these sentences.

1. The driver is/are driving fast.
2. Are/is these your storybooks?
3. We must eats/eat healthy food.
4. Children enjoys/enjoy birthday parties.
5. The doctor and the nurse are/is on duty.
6. They has/have a kitchen garden in the backyard.

Read these sentences carefully.

A table and **a** chair were in one corner.

There was **a** large door in **the** wall, which was **the** cupboard.

Grandfather was **an** old man who lived alone.

The words *a*, *an*, and *the* are called **articles**.

The article *a* is used before singular nouns that begin with a consonant sound.

Examples: **a** table, **a** chair, **a** door

The article *an* is used before singular nouns that begin with a vowel sound.

Examples: **an** old man, **an** apple, **an** hour

The article *the* refers to a particular person, place, or thing.

Examples: **the** cupboard, **the** goats, **the** first day, **the** Alps mountains

We use the articles *a* or *an* when we talk about something for the first time. When we speak about it again, we use *the*.

Examples: Ria picked **an apple**. She put **the apple** in her bag.

A boy was painting the gate. **The boy** finished after an hour.

Language Booster

We use *an* before a word that begins with a silent letter and the second letter is a vowel.

Example: an **hou**r

B. Fill in the blanks with *a*, *an*, or *the*.

1. Rakesh is ______ honest officer.
2. ______ sun set in ______ mountains.
3. There was ______ little girl selling flowers.
4. Heidi lived with her grandfather in ______ Alps.
5. I packed ______ sandwich and ______ orange for lunch.
6. Please carry ______ umbrella because it is raining outside.

Study Skills jumbled words

Spelling

Rearrange the letters to find words from the story.

1. PERCE: C________________
2. FLTO: L________________
3. SSREAC: C________________
4. TEARHH: H________________
5. PENSUDS: S________________
6. STLERU: R________________

Listening listening to a passage and gap filling

Listen to a passage about a boy and his grandfather. Then, choose the correct options to complete the sentences.

1. Sam and his grandfather were ________________.
   a. best friends b. enemies c. classmates
2. Every morning, together they went to ________________.
   a. the market b. the park c. the bus stop
3. At night, they ________________.
   a. cooked dinner b. chopped firewood c. shared jokes
4. As Sam failed to do his duties, Grandfather ________________.
   a. scolded him b. ignored him c. praised him
5. Sam understood that he should ________________.
   a. leave his grandfather
   b. listen to his grandfather
   c. do what he thought was right

Speaking making polite requests and thanking someone

21ST CENTURY Collaboration 21ST CENTURY Communication

Work in groups of six. Enact these conversations.

1. Imagine that you are seated around a table with five friends. Your noodle soup tastes bland. You want to add salt and pepper to the soup. The containers are a few seats away. Ask your neighbours for the containers.
2. You are having lunch with your family. The dessert at the end of the meal is delicious. Thank your aunt who made it.

Writing

describing the similarities and differences

Write two things that are the same and two things that are different in the two pictures.

Photograph 1

Photograph 2

Explore More

Read the story *Eight Cousins* by Louisa May Alcott. It is about Rose Campbell who, after becoming an orphan, has to live with her six aunts and seven mischievous cousins.

Watch the film *Annie*. Annie is an orphan and is adopted by a rich man. Everyone in the house grows to love her and 'Daddy' Warbucks helps her in finding her real parents.

UNIT VI Folktales

Warm-up

A. Work in groups of four. Name the folktales in which these characters or things appear. The first group to name all six correctly will be the winner.

1. ____________________

2. ____________________

3. ____________________

4. ____________________

5. ____________________

6. ____________________

B. Are you a good friend? Look at these pictures and say what you would do to be a good friend in each situation.

poem 13

The Lion and the Mouse

Paul King

Curricular Goals

- develop a comprehensive range of vocabulary in various contexts
- sustain effective communication skills for day-to-day interactions
- develop the ability to express themselves in writing

Competencies

- can pair rhyming words
- can write a dialogue and enact it

Reading

a *Do you think that the bigger an animal or a person is, the stronger they are? Read this poem, based on a well-known folktale, and find out whether a small mouse is able to help a mighty lion when he is in trouble.*

A lion lies sleeping, silent and **still**[1],
Along comes a mouse and thinks he's a hill.
Up the great body, the little mouse goes,
Through **mane**, across ear, and down Lion's nose.

But Lion wakes up and gives a great roar,
Catches poor Mouse in his long cruel **claw**.
'How dare you walk over your king and your Lord!
For this only death shall be your **reward**.'

The little mouse **shivers and shudders** with fright,
Tries hard to think how to put things **a-right**.
'Forgive my mistake, mighty Lion, I pray,
And I promise to help you too some day.'

At this Lion laughs and shakes **to and fro**,
But he's now **in good humour** and lets the mouse go.

Literary term

1. The sound of 's' is repeated in sleeping, silent, and still. This is an example of **alliteration**, where the same sound is repeated at the beginning of words placed close together.

still: without any movement
mane: the long thick hair that grows from a lion's neck
claw: sharp, curved nail on the end of an animal's or bird's foot
reward: something you get because of something good that you have done
shivers and shudders: shakes
a-right: all right
to and fro: moving repeatedly from one place to another and back again
in good humour: in a good mood

Common idioms and proverbs

A promise made is a promise kept: This proverb means that we must fulfil a promise we make.

Days come and days go, and some hunters pass by
Who set a great lion trap **cunning** and **sly**.
Lion walks in, **unaware of** the **threat**,
And suddenly finds himself caught in a net.

Helpless, he roars with **wrath** and **despair**;
Little Mouse hears how he's caught in a **snare**.
She remembers her promise and runs without **pause**
To the spot where the lion so **rages** and roars.

Her sharp little teeth set to **gnawing** the rope,
Thread after thread, now the Lion feels hope.
Soon there's a hole and the Lion is freed.
The mouse has kept her promise indeed!

cunning: (here) cleverly made
sly: (here) hidden
unaware of: without realising
threat: (here) danger
wrath: anger
despair: feeling of being without hope
snare: a trap for catching birds and animals
pause: (here) stopping
rages: roars in anger
gnawing: chewing

In a Nutshell

Who A playful mouse and a proud lion

When The mouse runs over the sleeping lion's body and wakes him up.

What The lion lets the mouse go. The mouse promises to help the lion.

How The mouse sets the lion free from the hunter's net.

About the poet

Paul King is from Britain but worked as a teacher in different countries. He has written many poems for children. He is now retired and settled in England.

Understanding the Poem

A. State whether the following sentences are true (T) or false (F). Rewrite the incorrect sentences correctly in your notebook.

1. The mouse climbed on top of the lion thinking it was a valley. ☐
2. When the lion woke up, he caught the mouse with his tail. ☐

3. The mouse promised to help the lion one day. ☐
4. Some villagers laid a trap for the lion. ☐
5. The mouse ran to help the lion when she heard his cries for help. ☐
6. The mouse cut through the net with her sharp claws. ☐
7. The mouse made a hole in the net through which the lion escaped. ☐
8. The mouse could not keep her promise. ☐

B. Read the lines and answer the questions.

1. *At this Lion laughs and shakes to and fro,*
   But he's now in good humour and lets the mouse go.
   a. Why did the lion laugh?
   b. What had the lion said he would do to the mouse? Why?
   c. Why did he let the mouse go?
2. *She remembers her promise and runs without pause*
   To the spot where the lion so rages and roars.
   a. Who is 'she' in these lines?
   b. What was the promise she made?
   c. Why was the lion raging and roaring?

Life Skills and Values

keeping a promise and emotions

21ST CENTURY Critical Thinking

1. Did the mouse keep her promise? Why do you think keeping one's promise is important?
2. Name three different emotions that the lion feels in the poem. Give lines from the poem to support your answer.

Vocabulary

rhyming words

Rhyming words are words which end with the same sound.

Examples: A lion lies sleeping, silent and **still**,
Along comes a mouse and thinks he's a **hill**.

The words *still* and *hill* end with the same sound. They are rhyming words.

Find two words from the poem which rhyme with each of these words. Add another rhyming word of your own.

1.	rose	nose	goes	pose
2.	bill			
3.	might			
4.	say			
5.	my			
6.	pet			

Activity

writing a dialogue, making and enacting it with sock puppets

Work in groups of four. Make sock puppets of the lion and the mouse. Then, use the lines from the poem to write an imaginary dialogue between the lion and the mouse. Act it out using the puppets.

You may begin this way:

How to make the sock puppets:

You will need:

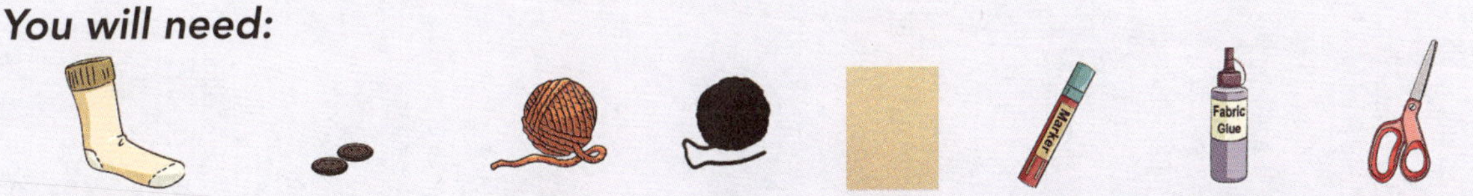

clean old socks (brown/ yellow and white/grey) | black buttons | light brown or red wool | thick black wool | felt paper | markers | fabric glue | scissors

Procedure:

1. To make the lion, take a light brown or yellow sock. Use a white or a grey sock to make the mouse.

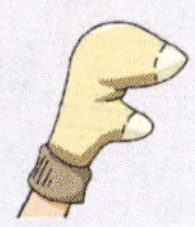

2. Slide your hand inside the sock. Fold and make a C-shape with your hand. Put your fingers into the toe area. Fit your thumb into the heel area.

3. Open and close your hand to practise how to make the puppet 'talk'.

4. Stick two black buttons to make the eyes.

5. Draw a triangle for the nose. Use a marker.

6. Use light brown wool to make the lion's mane.
   Stick it on the sock puppet using fabric glue.
   Cut out ears from felt paper and stick them on.

7. Make whiskers for the lion and mouse using the thick black wool and stick them on.

Your sock puppets are ready!

Explore More

Read the poem *The Fox and the Crow* by Paul King. It is based on the famous fable of the clever fox who tricks a proud crow.

Watch the film *Up*. It teaches us that no one is ever too young (or too old) to help someone else.

folktale

14

Gopal and the Hilsa Fish

Curricular Goals

- develop a comprehensive range of vocabulary in various contexts
- develop fluency in reading and the ability to read with comprehension
- sustain effective communication skills for day-to-day interactions
- develop the ability to express themselves in writing

Competencies

- can understand phrasal verbs and add different prefixes to form new words
- can identify the subject, verb, and object in a sentence, use apostrophe in contractions, and correct commonly misspelt words
- can talk on a topic for a minute and write a diary entry

Reading

a *Raja Krishnachandra was the king of Krishnanagar. Gopal was a courtier in his court. He was famous for his wit. Read this story to find out more.*

It was the season of **Hilsa fish** in Krishnanagar. Everyone spoke only about the fish. Raja Krishnachandra was **tired of** hearing his **courtiers** only talk about the fish.

So, one day he yelled, 'Will you all stop talking about the Hilsa fish?' The courtiers were surprised and became silent. The king realised that he may have **reacted** too soon. So, he said, 'I know it is Hilsa season, and no one can stop anyone from talking about it. So, I have a **challenge**. Can any one of you buy a Hilsa fish and bring it to the palace without being asked about it?'

Gopal, one of the king's courtiers said, 'I can make people stop talking about the fish. I accept this challenge!'

A few days later, Gopal **shaved** half his face, applied ash all over his body, and wore a pair of torn clothes.

Hilsa fish: an expensive and tasty fish, very popular in eastern parts of India, available in only certain seasons

tired of: (here) bored of

courtiers: men and women at the court of a king or queen

reacted: (here) behaved in a particular way because of a situation

challenge: something new and difficult which requires great effort

shaved: removed hair from the face

His wife was shocked to see him. She asked, 'Where are you going like this?'
He replied, 'I'm going to buy Hilsa fish.'
The poor woman thought, 'Oh no! How silly of him to go out like that!'
She stopped him. She said, 'I'll buy the fish. You stay at home.'
But Gopal did not listen to her and went to the market.

Where was Gopal going?

When he went out, nobody recognised Gopal. Everybody laughed and said, 'What a strange man!'

Gopal was not bothered by this. He bought the fish and walked to the palace. Nobody looked at or talked about the fish. They continued looking and talking about him.

'Look at that **comical** man!'

'Who is he?'

When Gopal reached the palace, the guards did not let him enter. He started singing loudly and dancing **wildly**. He made a lot of noise which **drew the attention** of Raja Krishnachandra. He asked his guards, 'Who is making so much noise? Send him in!'

As Gopal entered the king's court, one of the courtiers recognised him and said, 'Wait! This is Gopal.'

Why did the people laugh at Gopal?

Everyone was **stunned**. The king asked, 'Gopal, what is the meaning of this? Why are you dressed like this? Is this another joke?'

Gopal smiled and said, 'Your Majesty, do you remember the challenge? Today, I bought a Hilsa fish and walked all the way here. Nobody asked me about the fish.'

Everyone burst into laughter. Raja Krishnachandra remembered the challenge and said, 'Well done, Gopal. You are a clever man indeed! Congratulations on winning the challenge.'

comical: funny or silly
wildly: (here) in an uncontrolled way
drew the attention: made (someone) notice something
stunned: shocked

In a Nutshell

Who Gopal, the witty courtier and Raja Krishnachandra

What Gopal accepted the challenge to buy a Hilsa fish and bring it to the court, without anyone talking about it.

When In the season of Hilsa fish

How By distracting everyone's attention from the fish

Cross-curricular Corner

Folktales are stories told by 'folk' and about 'folk'. The word 'folk' means the people. They are stories about people's lives and customs passed on from one generation to another by word of mouth.

Comprehension

A. State whether the sentences are true (T) or false (F).

1. Everyone talked about Hilsa because it was the season of Hilsa fish. ☐
2. The king lost his temper because he was tired of eating Hilsa fish. ☐
3. The king wanted someone to buy a Hilsa fish and bring it to court. ☐
4. Gopal was a poor and silly person. ☐
5. The king was impressed with Gopal for dressing up strangely to court. ☐
6. No one talked about the fish because Gopal's appearance distracted them. ☐

B. Read the lines and answer the questions.

1. *Will you all stop talking about the Hilsa fish?*
   a. Who said this?
   b. How was the speaker feeling when he said this?
   c. Why was everyone talking about the Hilsa fish?
2. *I'll buy the fish. You stay at home.*
   a. Who said these words and to whom?
   b. Why did the speaker ask the other person to stay at home?
   c. Who was the speaker buying the fish for?
3. *Look at that comical man!*
   a. Who said these words and to whom?
   b. What was comical about the man?
   c. Where was the comical man headed to? How do you know?

Life Skills and Values

finding solutions

1. During a test in class, your pencil breaks. You don't have a spare one and you are not allowed to talk. How will you handle such a situation?
2. Can you think of another way to win the king's challenge?

Vocabulary

phrasal verbs

A. Fill in the blanks with the correct phrasal verbs from the box.

lived on	make money	flew away	get hurt

1. The poor man found a clever way to ______________ and soon became rich.
2. The birds got scared by the noise of bursting crackers and ______________.
3. You might ______________ if you are not careful with the big scissors.
4. The farmer ______________ the money he made by selling his crops.

prefixes: *un-*, *in-*, *dis-*

We can change the meaning of a word by adding letters before them to make a new word.

Examples: forgettable → **un**forgettable

dependent → **in**dependent

obey → **dis**obey

The new word may be opposite in meaning to the old word.

B. Add *un-*, *in-*, or *dis-* to form new words.

1. ____true
2. ____agree
3. ____correct
4. ____kind
5. ____certain
6. ____appear
7. ____able
8. ____visible
9. ____complete

Grammar

subject–verb–object

You have learnt about subject and predicate in a sentence.

Look at these sentences.

I accept this challenge.
(subject: *I*; verb: *accept*)

She stopped him.
(subject: *She*; verb: *stopped*)

The object usually comes after the verb in a sentence and is a noun or a pronoun.

To find the object in the sentence, we ask the question *What?* or *Whom?* after the verb.

Question: I accept what? **Answer:** *this challenge*

So, *this challenge* is the object of the verb *accept* in sentence 1.

Question: She stopped whom? **Answer:** *him*

Him is the object of the verb *stopped* in sentence 2.

A. Circle the subjects, underline the verbs, and write the objects.

1. (We) met the actor. the actor
2. Sushil was flying a kite. ____________
3. The girl loves mangoes. ____________
4. The boy played the guitar. ____________
5. The policeman caught the thief. ____________
6. The carpenter made a cupboard. ____________

apostrophe in contractions

Read these sentences.

I'm going to buy Hilsa fish.

Gopal **wasn't** bothered by this.

In these sentences, *I'm* is formed by joining *I* and *am*. *Wasn't* is formed by joining *was* and *not*.

We use an **apostrophe** (') to show the dropped letter when we join two words and shorten them.

B. Write the short forms for these words using an apostrophe.

1. do not ________
2. let us ________
3. will not ________
4. it is ________
5. you are ________
6. could not ________

Study Skills

Spelling

correcting common mistakes

Circle the correctly spelt word.

1.	challange	challenge	challeng
2.	accepted	exepted	aceppted
3.	yeled	yeld	yelled
4.	discussed	discused	discussd
5.	appleid	applyed	applied
6.	dressd	dressed	dresd

Listening

listening to a folktale for details

Listen to a story about Emperor Akbar and his favourite minister, Birbal, and choose the correct options.

1. What did Birbal do after leaving Akbar's kingdom?
   a. He started selling vegetables.
   b. He started working on a farm.
   c. He started his own jewellery business.
2. Why did Akbar miss Birbal?
   a. He found it difficult to solve problems without Birbal's help.
   b. He did not have a partner to play chess.
   c. He was not happy with his other ministers.
3. What did Akbar ask the head of every village to send him?
   a. A pot filled with wit
   b. A pot filled with food
   c. A pot filled with fruits
4. What did Birbal send the Emperor?
   a. Gold jewels in a pot
   b. A watermelon in a pot
   c. A book of jokes in a pot

Speaking

extempore speaking / just a minute (JAM)

Talk about a festival or a special day that you want to celebrate.

You can speak about these:

- when this day/festival is celebrated
- how many times it comes in a month/year/few years

- how this day/festival is usually celebrated
- what special foods are made
- how you will celebrate it

Writing

writing a diary entry

21ST CENTURY Creativity

Imagine you are the king of Krishnanagar. Write what you feel about the events in the story in the form of a diary entry.

You can write about these:

- the Hilsa season in the kingdom
- everyone talking about fish
- the challenge to your courtier, Gopal
- how you feel when Gopal comes with the fish

Don't forget to add the date to the entry. Here is a sample format.

14 March

Dear diary,

It is the Hilsa season in my kingdom and ...

____

____

____

____

____

____

____

____

____

____

____

____

____

____

____

____

____

____

____

____

Explore More

Read the book *Grandma's Bag of Stories* by Sudha Murthy. It is a collection of short stories and Indian folktales.

Watch the video *Birth of Ganesha* by Amar Chitra Katha. It is the story of the birth and rise of Ganesha.

short story

15 True Friends

Curricular Goals

- develop a comprehensive range of vocabulary in various contexts
- develop fluency in reading and the ability to read with comprehension
- sustain effective communication skills for day-to-day interactions
- develop the ability to express themselves in writing

→

Competencies

- can understand synonyms, use *get*, *make*, *have*, and *let*, identify different tenses of verbs, and make simple commands and instructions
- can identify and say the sounds of *v* and *w*
- can give simple instructions and write a narrative paragraph

Reading

a *The great king of Vijaynagar, Krishna Deva Raya, had many wise ministers in his court. Tenali Raman was the wisest of them all. He was also popular for his wit. Read this story about the way Tenali Raman solves an unusual problem.*

One morning at King Krishna Deva Raya's court, two men entered carrying a golden statue of a swan. All the courtiers were **awestruck** by the beauty of the statue. It was **studded** with diamonds and **precious** stones, which **glittered** in the light. The richness of the statue was **in stark contrast** to the poor **appearance** of the two men.

'Who are you and what do you want in our court?' asked the King.

'Maharaj, my name is Ramu and this is my best friend, Shamu. We have been best friends and neighbours since childhood. He grows vegetables and I am a rice farmer. In last month's sudden rains, most of his harvest was destroyed and his fields became **waterlogged**.'

How did Ramu and Shamu know each other?

awestruck: amazed
studded: decorated
precious: worth a lot of money
glittered: shone
in stark contrast: opposite to
appearance: the way someone looks
waterlogged: full of water

Shamu continued: 'Like a good friend, Ramu helped me in my time of need. He offered me a section of his land where I could plant some fast-growing vegetables. Yesterday I was **tilling** the land. Suddenly, I found this golden swan.'

'Shamu came to me with the statue at once. He says that since the statue was found in my land, it belongs to me,' said Ramu.

'I think that giving it to him was the right thing to do,' said Shamu.

'But he was the one who found the statue. I think it belongs to him. But I can't make him take it,' complained Ramu.

What kind of cases did the king's court usually get?

'Very interesting,' Krishna Deva Raya said. He was **amused**. He had never come across such a case.

'Who can settle the **dispute** between these two friends? Whom does the swan belong to?' asked Krishna Deva Raya to his courtiers. 'It looks like neither will accept it.'

It was a strange situation. Usually the disputes that came to the king's court involved people fighting over riches and land. This was exactly the opposite. Each friend wanted to gift the swan to the other.

The court priest, Chatur Pandit, spoke: 'Dear King, this swan has been found in the **earth** of this kingdom. It is a sign from the gods. Please give me permission to take this golden statue home and **inspect** it. Then I can **consult** the religious books and do the necessary **rituals** for the well-being of the king and the kingdom.'

Cross-curricular Corner

Chatur means 'clever' in Sanskrit and several other Indian languages. It suggests the kind of person the court pandit is.

Everyone in the courtroom understood that this was Chatur Pandit's cunning plan to steal some of the diamonds and gems from the statue. After his 'inspection' was over, the swan would lose most of its valuable stones.

The king's **treasurer** spoke next: 'Your Majesty, I think the swan belongs to the royal **treasury**. We should keep it.'

What did the king's treasurer want to do with the swan?

Krishna Deva Raya shook his head. He disagreed with these ideas. He turned to his wise and witty minister Tenali Raman.

'Tenali, let me hear your idea.'

tilling: digging the land to grow crops
amused: thought that something was funny
dispute: disagreement
earth: (here) land
inspect: to look carefully
consult: to check
rituals: ceremonies
treasurer: someone who is in charge of the money and accounts
treasury: place where money and riches are kept

'Your Highness, I think we should **auction** this swan. The money we get from it should be used to build a beautiful garden in the main street of the kingdom. It should have a freshwater fountain and shady trees. Travellers from around the world should get to rest there. We should have a tall pillar in the middle of the garden with the wonderful story of these **generous** friends **engraved** on it. Thus, their great friendship will be remembered for generations to come.'

Both the friends were very pleased to hear this suggestion. The king and the courtiers praised Tenali Raman for thinking about the good of everybody.

auction: to sell to the person who pays the highest price

generous: kind and giving

engraved: words or designs cut on stone or wood

In a Nutshell

Who Two friends Ramu and Shamu

What They sought the king's help to settle their dispute.

How Tenali Raman, the king's minister, found a solution that made everyone happy.

Comprehension

A. State whether the sentences are true (T) or false (F). Write the false sentences correctly in your notebook.

1. One morning at King Krishna Deva Raya's court, three men entered carrying a golden statue of a swan. ☐
2. Ramu grew vegetables and Shamu was a rice farmer. ☐
3. Shamu discovered the statue while watering his crops. ☐
4. Chatur Pandit wanted to take the statue to his temple. ☐
5. The minister thought that the swan belonged to the treasury. ☐
6. Tenali Raman thought that they should hide the swan. ☐

B. Read the lines and answer the questions.

1. *Dear King, this swan has been found in the earth of this kingdom.*
   a. Who said these words? Who was he?
   b. What permission did he want?
   c. What did the courtiers realise?
2. *Your Highness, I think we should auction this swan.*
   a. Who said these words and to whom?
   b. What would they do with the money from auctioning the swan?
   c. Why did the speaker suggest this plan?
   d. What did the others think of the plan?

Life Skills and Values

friendship and generosity

21ST CENTURY Critical Thinking

1. What do you think of the friendship between Ramu and Shamu? What do you learn from their bond?
2. What kind of a person was Chatur Pandit? Do you think he was honest?

Vocabulary

synonyms

A. Circle the option which is the closest in meaning to the words from the story.

1. **awestruck**	a. silent	b. scared	c. amazed
2. **destroy**	a. build	b. ruin	c. take
3. **dispute**	a. solution	b. disagreement	c. agreement
4. **pleased**	a. happy	b. sad	c. excited
5. **waterlogged**	a. soaked	b. flooded	c. wet
6. **valuable**	a. rich	b. expensive	c. cheap

using *get, make, have, let*

Read these sentences. Look at the way the verbs *get, make, have,* and *let* can be used.

Travellers from around the world should **get** to rest there.

But I can't **make** him take it.

It should **have** a freshwater fountain and shady trees.

Tenali, **let** me hear your idea.

B. Fill in the blanks with the correct options.

1. I _____________ (let/have) a lot of homework to finish.
2. Let us _____________ (get/have) a party for Children's Day.
3. I am going to _____________ (get/make) my room painted.
4. Mother will _____________ (let/have) me watch cartoons today.
5. The teacher will _____________ (make/get) Rajan learn his lines.
6. The school will _____________ (get/let) students take part in inter-school competitions.

Grammar

present continuous tense

Read these sentences.

I **am waiting** for someone in court to settle this dispute.

The teacher **is writing** on the board.

The verbs *am waiting* and *is writing* are in the present continuous tense.

The **present continuous tense** describes actions or events which are happening now or at the time of speaking.

A. Fill in the blanks with the present continuous tense of the verbs given in brackets.

Sunil's mother _______________ (prepare) cereal for the entire family. Sunil _______________ (wear) his uniform in his room. His father _______________ (call) him for breakfast. His sister _______________ (eat) only toast for breakfast and their mother _______________ (get) angry with her. The twins _______________ (pack) their bags now. There is complete confusion. Suddenly, the school van arrives. The children _______________ (yell) in the van.

Read this sentence.

Shamu **was tilling** the land.

The verb *was tilling* is in the past continuous tense.

The **past continuous tense** describes actions or events which began in the past and continued for some time.

Look at some more examples.

Ramu and Shamu **were carrying** a golden statue when they entered.

The birds **were singing** in the trees.

B. Identify the sentences which are in the past continuous tense and underline the verbs.

1. The boy is drawing with a pencil.
2. Shaheen was making a model aeroplane.
3. The princess was wearing golden slippers.
4. Arvind is making breakfast for his parents today.
5. Rani's mother was buying her a dress for her birthday.
6. Shamu was giving the swan to Ramu as it was the right thing to do.

Read these sentences.

If you grant me permission, I **will inspect** the statue.

I **will go** to school tomorrow.

The verbs *will inspect* and *will go* are in the simple future tense.

The **simple future tense** describes an action that will happen some time in the future.

ia **C. Fill in the blanks with the simple future tense of the verbs given in brackets.**

1. I ______________________ (clean) my room tomorrow.
2. I ______________________ (complete) the report tonight.

3. My mother ____________________ (knit) a sweater for me.
4. Rama ____________________ (dance) in the competition next week.
5. The king ____________________ (go) to the race tomorrow morning.
6. The carpenter ____________________ (complete) his work in two days.

simple commands and instructions

Read these sentences.

Finish your work.

Sit down and **open** your notebook.

Don't make a noise.

These sentences tell someone to do or not to do something. These are simple commands or instructions.

ia **D. Fill in the blanks with the correct words from the box.**

clean	run	study	step	come

1. Don't __________ in the corridor.
2. __________ in. You don't have to knock.
3. Don't __________ on the carpet with shoes on.
4. __________ regularly if you want to do well in school.
5. __________ the blackboard before the next class begins.

Study Skills

Pronunciation

sounds of *v* and *w*

A. Listen to the sounds of *v* and *w* in these words from the story. Say the words aloud. Pay attention to the difference in their sounds.

vegetable   water   valuable   world

B. Now, listen to six words that have either the *v* or the *w* sound in them. Circle the correct sound for each.

1. v w   2. v w   3. v w   4. v w   5. v w   6. v w

Listening

identifying polite and rude commands

Listen to the sentences and identify the polite and the rude commands. Give reasons for choosing them.

Speaking

giving simple instructions

In groups of four, enact a scenario out of the given sentences. Each group will get four sentences. Speak using the correct tone for the situation.

- Bring me a glass of water.
- Don't ever touch my phone.
- Give me a pen and a pencil.
- Play. It's your turn.
- Remember what I told you!
- Don't be excited about everything without reason.
- Don't rush or you will fall.
- Read a lot to improve your writing skills.

The first sentence (*Bring me a glass of water.*) could be said by the father to the mother, a doctor to the attendant, the sister to the brother, etc.

Writing

writing a narrative paragraph

Write a paragraph about a memorable incident with your best friend.

You can include the following points:

- what the incident was about
- when and where it happened
- if you were happy or sad afterwards
- how your friend felt

Explore More

Read *The Great Tenali Rama*. This is a collection of stories about Tenali Rama and his experiences at the court of King Krishna Deva Raya. They show his wit and cleverness.

Watch the film *Tenali Raman* on YouTube.

Project 3

A. You read about Heidi's growing bond with her grandfather. Now, conduct an interview with your grandparents and write a story on their childhood for your school newspaper or magazine.

You could include the following points:

- details of their childhood (the place where they grew up, their school, hobbies)
- a special childhood memory of theirs
- how things were different when they were young

Remember to give a catchy title to your story.

21st Century Creativity · 21st Century Collaboration

SCHOOL SPOTLIGHT

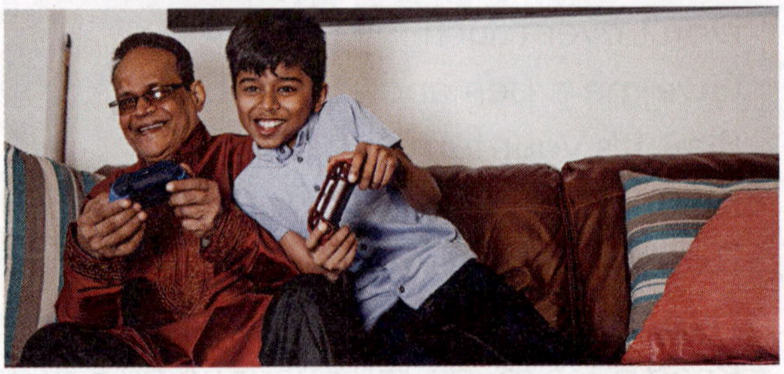

MY GRANDFATHER, MY SUPERHERO!

EXCLUSIVE INTERVIEW

Raghav: Hello, sir. Please tell us a little bit about your school life.

Grandfather: I was born in Chennai. I went to a school called Lawrence High School.

Raghav: What were your favourite subjects?

Grandfather: My favourite subjects were English and Maths.

Raghav: Please share a special memory.

Grandfather: I once broke the neighbour's window while playing cricket. He was very angry!

WHY HE IS MY BEST FRIEND

My grandfather is my best friend and superhero. He plays with me and takes me out on long walks. He knows a lot. He helps me with my school work and talks to me about sports, films, and what's on the news. He tells me jokes and plays board games with me and my friends. He also shares my hobbies.

B. You read 'Paplu, the Giant', which has magic elements. Now, choose a storybook that has magical characters or events. Write a book review.

You may choose from any one of these books:

- *The Magic Faraway Tree* by Enid Blyton
- *The Wonderful Wizard of Oz* by L. Frank Baum
- *Peter Pan* by J. M. Barrie
- *The Wind in the Willows* by Kenneth Grahame

My Book Review

Title of the book:

Author:

Main characters:
Other characters:
What the story is about:
What I like about the book:
Number of stars I would like to give the book: ☆☆☆☆☆